TRICKS
of the
ACTIVE
TRADER

TRICKS

of the

ACTIVE
TRADER

An Insider's Techniques
for Getting the Edge

NEAL T. WEINTRAUB

McGRAW-HILL

*New York   Chicago   San Francisco   Lisbon   London   Madrid   Mexico City
Milan   New Delhi   San Juan   Seoul   Singapore   Sydney   Toronto*

The *McGraw-Hill* Companies

1 2 3 4 5 6 7 8 9 0   DOC/DOC   0 9 8 7 6

ISBN-13 978-0-07-146863-3
ISBN-10   0-07-146863-3

This publication is designed to provided accurate and authoritative information in regard to the subject matter covered. It is sold with the understanding that neither the author nor the publisher is engaged in rendering legal, accounting, or other professional service. If legal advice or other expert assistance is required, the services of a competent professional person should be sought.

—From a Declaration of Principles jointly adopted by Committee of the American Bar Association and a Committee of Publishers.

McGraw-Hill books are available at special quantity discounts to use a premiums and sales promotions, or for use in corporate training programs. For more information, please write to the Director of Special Sales, McGraw-Hill Professional, Two Penn Plaza, New York, NY 10121-2298. Or contact your local bookstore.

Library of Congress Cataloging-in-Publication Data

Weintraub, Neal.
  Tricks of the active trader : an insider's techniques for getting the edge / by Neal T. Weintraub.
        p. cm.
    ISBN 0-07-146863-3 (hardcover : alk. paper) 1. Electronic trading of securities. 2. Speculation. 3. Stocks. I. Title.
    HG4515.95.W44 2006
    332.64--dc22   2006015511

Contents

Tips

Traps

PART 2

Hardware, Operations, Software, and the Internet

Hardware Tips

Tricks

Traps

Operations Tips

Tricks

Traps

Software

The Internet
Tips

Tricks

Traps

PART 3

Trader's Notebook

Trader's Notebook 1

Trader's Notebook 2

Trader's Notebook 3

Trader's Notebook 4

Trader's Notebook 5

Trader's Notebook 6

Trader's Notebook 7

Trader's Notebook 8

Foreword

In February, Neal and I were in New York for a meeting and, as luck would have it, it was two days after the biggest snow storm in New York's history. As you can imagine, the normally 20- to 30-minute cab ride form LaGuardia to Midtown took an hour and a half. With the conversation pertaining to the impending meeting exhausted, Neal abruptly changed the subject by announcing that he was in the final stages of writing his latest book, *Tricks of the Active Trader*. My initial reaction was, "Not another how to day trade book." Neal assured me it was not another day trade book, and, after reviewing it, I agree.

I like this book because Neal's concept is there is not one way to trade. He writes that a trader should be active, and reminds the reader that active can mean doing nothing. You act, when you do nothing, by making the conscious (hopefully informed) decision to take no action. Many years ago, when I was just starting my trading career on the floor of the Chicago Board of Trade, one of the venerable traders told me that, more often than not, it was good business not to do business.

The meaning of "trading" has changed over the years. During that same cab ride Neal showed me a notebook that his father, who was a prisoner of war during World War II, had kept during his imprisonment. The U.S. prisoners were allowed to read books that were sent by the Red Cross. One of the books Neal's father read, and made notes about, was a book on investing that was first wirtten in 1933 and a second edition in 1939. From reading the notes I realized that in 1940 trading really didn't exist. Although there was a small group of traders on the BOT and the CME, the global economic impact of their efforts was minor and very few people, even in Chicago, were aware of their existence. Reading the notebook I realized that, at the time, speculating meant buying an undervalued stock and holding on for years. The word "trading" was not even used. During the ensuing 70 years trading has become part of the lexicon of investing. Obviously, markets have changed dramatically. Markets are now global, and information travels in nanoseconds. The Internet, TV, telephone communications, electronic trading, etc. have geometrically increased the speed and breadth of the dissemination of information, and the sheer number of markets available to trade throughout the world is growing exponentially.

You have to take control of your finances. As recent history has shown, there is no more relying on pensions for your retirement. Reading this book will not leave you with specific rules for financial success. Rather, the book focuses on the proper mind-set an individual must possess in order to achieve success in today's markets. I suspect that sometime in the latter half of this century someone will read this book, much as I read Neal's father's notebook, and be amazed how the markets of that time have so dramatically changed from today.

Laurence M. Rosenberg
Chairman
Lake Shore Group of Companies
www.lakeshorefunds.com
September 2006

Introduction

In a letter between fellow scientists, Isaac Newton wrote to Robert Hooke on February 5, 1676, modestly claiming that his success had been built on the achievements of others: "If I have seen further it is by standing on the shoulders of giants."

If I have seen further, it has been by observing traders, speaking with them, and learning with mixed results about their tricks, tips, traps, and techniques.

Besides standing among trading giants, I have been privileged to be with firms such as MTV, Nickelodeon, the Disney Channel, and the Chicago Board of Trade, along with the Movie Channel and the National Association of Realtors.

Today, with gutted pension funds, massive layoffs, and inflation, investors are taking an active role in protecting and advancing their financial portfolios. The days of corporate America being your financial partner are gone.

Unfortunately, I also have observed munchkins masquerading as titans of industry and traders confusing luck with skill. Many firms have imploded because of the greed, avarice, and incompetence of senior managers with "top tier" educational credentials, Ponzi personalities, designer suits, and the obligatory Rolex or Piaget.

The collateral damage from this unbridled use of corporate greed would make the great magician Harry Houdini jealous. Pension plans and dreams of a happy retirement, money for college tuition, and dignity in one's golden years have vanished like simple prestidigitations. What once took months now occurs in weeks.

Why be an active trader? Because of the *Titanic* effect. As Kenneth E.F. Watt once said, "The magnitude of disasters decreases to the extent that people believe that they are possible and maximize the effect."

We will have another market disaster. Plan for it. You must.

There may not be shoulders to stand on. You may not even be standing on your feet.

If you are curious about adding computer firepower to your trading, this book will point the way.

Patrick Young told a group of traders at the Chicago Mercantile Exchange: "But what you've got to bear in mind is, very quickly, your cost base can explode on you. And like I was saying yesterday, what you really need is a couple of PCs. One that does your entry and does your transactions, one that does your analytics and gets you onto the Internet and gets you research and gets you news. You need to have one with some sort of analytic software or perhaps a couple of pieces of analytical software, depending on what sort of analytics you are going to employ . . . whether it's technical analysis, whatever. But what you don't want to do is sit there and buy a huge amount of stuff. One of the biggest follies I've seen in a lot of electronic traders is they can sit down and end up with anything up to a several thousand if not $5,000 a month overhead before they go anywhere. And frankly, they don't need that stuff. Okay?"

To be brutally honest, you're better off starting with a relatively minimal amount of stuff and, as you find a need for something, adding to it. As long as you've got reasonable price data and as long as you've got a reasonable quantity of analytical software, whether it's a simple technical analysis package or anything like it, you can start trading.

Being an "active trader" has nothing to do with kinetic energy and everything to do with control. Your being in control.

In my view, individuals are taking charge of their own portfolios even as brokers claim that they not only will give advice but also insist on trading the investor's funds. If it doesn't work out, it's not the broker who loses; it's going to be you.

Being an active trader will not ensure your financial success. All motion is not progress, and spinning your wheels just burns rubber and gasoline.

Remember the tortoise and the hare? Who won the race?

If you are too active a trader, I hope this book will aid in honing your trading skills and help you evaluate your style of trading.

Using the Barbells

At a recent seminar on computer trading, Jim Oliff, vice chairman of the board of directors for the Mercantile Exchange, noted that the first item you should know about trading is yourself.

What is your motivation for trading?

Do you have the experience, knowledge, stamina, and capital for aggressive active trading?

One of the most difficult assignments I give students is to write a trading plan. If you can't write it out, you most likely don't have one. And without a plan, you are at the mercy of the unpredictable nature of the markets.

As you move along the path to becoming an active trader, a coherent written plan is vital.

Creating an investment portfolio or a trading plan is not a one-time event. You may have created a portfolio, but the financial market changes. No doubt your personal goals, risk tolerance, and time horizons also change.

Thus, if goals, risk tolerance, and time horizons are part of your trading decision making, you will trade less frequently than a trader who trades to earn an income.

For this reason we have constructed a linear bar for each trick of the active trader. We call these illustrations barbells.

No activity. Doesn't even think about trading or investing. The market is a grocery store.

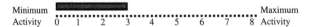

Usually a long-term investor. Maybe does one trade a year. Relies on a pension or a 401(k). Does not pay much attention to investing or trading. Too complacent.

Checks portfolio. Has a balanced approach but usually has no plan or strategy.

Has an interest in trading. Pays attention to the newspapers. May prefer other investments.

Reads about trading and is ready to pull the trigger. Looks at trading as another investment vehicle. Subscribes to a paper that has stock quotes.

Mixes investing with short-term trading. Pulls the trigger. Knows the difference between investing and trading.

Has a computer. Uses various front-end systems. Usually has no backup for hardware.

Trades for an income or does it as a full-time job. State-of-the-art trader. Has low brokerage rates. Has an objective.

Hyperactive trader on steroids. Walks a thin line between trading and gambling. This person is one step below a kamikaze pilot. A trading addict.

Part 1

Tricks, Tips, Traps, and Prestidigitation

Trick 1

Why Are You Here?

Minimum   Maximum
Activity   0   1   2   3   4   5   6   7   8   Activity

Why are you here? This is not a trick question. Are you here to prove you are right when it comes to trading? Are you trying to create a diversified portfolio? Or maybe you want to brag about being a trader. Why are you here?

There is only one reason: *To make money.* Sorry, no other reason will do. But if you are here to make money, why are you staying with losers that rob you of your capital?

Being wrong is part of trading. Staying wrong is a disaster.

The next time you place a trade, enter a stop-loss order with your broker.

I don't care if the broker doesn't ask you for one. You must do it. Now, I am not the brightest bulb on the tree, but I know this: You can have the most sophisticated algorithmic programs in the world, but without a stop-loss, a person tossing a quarter or throwing darts at the stock pages will beat you. (Thanks to Ron Paul for that comment.)

This goes for stocks, options, derivatives, and bonds. If you cannot admit when you are wrong and exit a trade, you will be carried out. All the software in the world cannot eliminate the emotional tendency to take losses in a personal way. It is not personal. It is just trading. Take the emotion out of it. Get the nikhedonia session over with before you trade.

3

"Need a friend? Buy a dog." That's from the movie *Wall Street*.

If you are trading to make yourself happy, it will not work. Think of the happiest moments in your life. How many of them revolved around money?

When you take a position in any trade, you immediately generate an emotional attachment. If I ask your opinion, you will give me one.

Next time say, "I have no opinion, I have a trading plan. I plan my trades and trade my plan." The only thing you can predict with certainty is the next cover of Oprah Winfrey's magazine. *Hint*: It's all about the "O."

If you want to buy with pride and hold with confidence, your chances of making it financially will decrease. An active trader does sit through a bear market, but with fixed income, not securities.

The media darling Suze Orman, with $24 million in zero-coupon bonds, can do that.

Terry Savage and Jane Bryant Quinn, who advocates buying an age-appropriate fund and getting on with one's life, will never worry about retirement.

Gosh, those folks will live off the interest on their interest.

It's up to you. Be an active trader and take control of your financial future or turn it over to someone you trust.

Being active does not mean doing day trading. Being active means taking control. It means flipping off the autopilot and taking control of the plane. As they say in the TD Waterhouse commercial, "You can do this."

Your nescience about trading is no excuse. The information is out there. And don't be lazy, or crazy.

Trick 2

Precious Metals Are a Must for Your Portfolio

Minimum 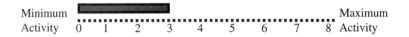 Maximum
Activity 0   1   2   3   4   5   6   7   8 Activity

A little gold in your portfolio is a trick more big hedge funds are using these days, and now that Arthur Hailey's *The Moneychangers* is being rereleased, gold should take on a new luster. This is the book that *Business Week* called "absolutely delicious ... really hard to put down." When it first was published, it rocked the banking world, exposing a level of greed that permeated nearly every sector of banking from back room to boardroom. That was 25 years ago.

In a new foreword by the author, Hailey poses the question, "Financially, and banking-wise, have things changed since my gold novel?" His answer: *"Absolutely!* Now, much worse and the amounts of money involved and endangered substantially greater."

Hailey's book follows the path of two characters jockeying for the position of chairman of an established bank when its founder dies. Then decisions endangering the client's money are made to boost one competitor's chances, with rippling effects. Characters are threatened, jailed, displaced. Decisions prompted by ambition teeter atop a company with links to the bank, cross-directorships— a financial house of cards.

In a passage in the book that is as controversial and thought-provoking today as it was a quarter of a century ago, an executive screams about the need to return to gold: "Gold as a base, once more, for the world's money systems. Gold, the oldest, the only bastion of monetary integrity. Gold, the one source, incorruptible, of fiscal discipline. Gold, which politicians cannot print … which, because of its severely limited supply, establishes its own real, lasting value."

I am certainly no gold bug, but I don't think there is anything wrong with having access to silver or gold coins. Also, I believe that there are artificial forces keeping the price of gold at low levels. Certainly, on the spectrum of investing, gold does not get touted. However, that is changing.

If you are going to invest, why not take a broader approach and consider Vanguard's precious metals fund? This way you are exposed to the entire mining industry.

Here is a partial list of precious metals funds for your consideration. You also can purchase metals and store them. Add to that options and gold mining stocks, and you can go, as they say, hogwild. You can also day trade gold as a futures contract, use the Internet, and visit the Chicago Board of Trade. You will see a live book of actual gold and silver trades. However, unless you really have a trading strategy, start with mutual funds. There is also a Web site that really drills down into the mining market: Free MarketNewsNetwork.Com. In the interest of disclosure, I do not own any of the funds mentioned here. However, for years I did own Vanguard's precious metals fund. It is currently closed to new subscribers. Your precious metals fund must beat the stock market indexes and the Treasury rates on a year-end basis. If it does not, sell it.

Fund Name	Symbol
ProFunds Precious Metals Ultra Inv	PMPIX
ProFunds Precious Metals Ultra Svc	PMPSX

Fund Name	Symbol
U.S. Global Investors WrldPrecMineral	UNWPX
U.S. Global Investors Gold Shares	USERX
Van Eck Intl Investors Gold A	INIVX
Van Eck Intl Investors Gold C	IIGCX
American Century Global Gold Inv	BGEIX
American Century Global Gold Adv	ACGGX
Evergreen Precious Metals I	EKWYX
Evergreen Precious Metals A	EKWA
ProFunds Precious Metals Ultra Inv	PMPIX
ProFunds Precious Metals Ultra Svc	PMPSX
Midas	MIDSX
Franklin Gold and Precious Metals Adv	FGADX
Franklin Gold and Precious Metals A	FKRCX
Franklin Gold and Precious Metals C	FRGOX
Franklin Gold and Precious Metals B	FAGPX
U.S. Global Investors Gold Shares	USERX
Van Eck Intl Investors Gold A	INIVX
Van Eck Intl Investors Gold C	IIGCX
U.S. Global Investors WrldPrecMineral	UNWPX
Vanguard Precious Metals and Mining	VGPMX
U.S. Global Investors Gold Shares	USERX
Evergreen Precious Metals I	EKWYX
Evergreen Precious Metals A	EKWAX
Scudder Gold & Precious Metals AARP	SGLDX
Scudder Gold & Precious Metals S	SCGDX
Scudder Gold & Precious Metals A	SGDAX
Evergreen Precious Metals B	EKWBX

(Continued)

Fund Name	Symbol
Evergreen Precious Metals C	EKWCX
U.S. Global Investors WrldPrecMineral	UNWPX
Evergreen Precious Metals I	EKWYX
Evergreen Precious Metals A	EKWAX
USAA Precious Metals and Minerals	USAGX
First Eagle Gold A	SGGDX
U.S. Global Investors Gold Shares	USERX
GAMCO Gold AAA	GOLDX
Tocqueville Gold	TGLDX

Your securities broker can assist you in purchasing any of these funds. The funds also may be used as part of a retirement plan.

Trick 3

Market Access: Does Faster and Cheaper Always Trump Slower and More Expensive?

By Barrett Fiske

Barrett D. Fiske is a commodity trading advisor and the president of Fiske Walter Capital Management Ltd. (FWCM), which he cofounded in January 2004. During the period of interest rate volatility in the early 1990s, Fiske was a two-year-basis arbitrage trader who routinely carried positions in excess of $400 million. During the meteoric rise in the U.S. equity markets in the late 1990s, he traded the extremely lucrative Nasdaq basis.

Currently, in addition to his duties as head trader for FWCM, for which he primarily trades foreign currency and U.S. equity spreads, Fiske is a consultant to individual traders and hedge fund traders as well as to brokerage firms. He is also a regular special subjects teacher for the member-traders at the Chicago Mercantile Exchange (CME).

Minimum Activity 0 1 2 3 4 5 6 7 8 Maximum Activity

Without question, the biggest change in the futures industry in the past 25 years has been in market access. If you were a retail investor back in 1980, the only way you could make a trade was to pick up the phone and call your broker.

Here's how it used to work: You call the brokerage firm, and a receptionist answers and passes you through to your broker. You

9

tell the broker what you want to do, specifying the commodity, the expiration month, and the price at which you want to buy or sell. The broker time stamps and writes up an order ticket and then records your voice confirmation of the order. He or she then delivers your order ticket to an order desk. The person at the order desk calls a clerk at an order desk on the exchange floor and repeats your order, getting a voice recording of the floor clerk's confirmation. The floor clerk then writes up the order, time stamps it, and hands it to a runner. The runner delivers your order to a pit clerk, who hands it off to a broker, who offers it out to the pit. After another floor broker or a floor trader takes the other side of your order, the report of your filled order follows the same track in reverse, culminating in a call back to you from your broker with the completed execution.

Today that whole process is accomplished in one keystroke.

The ramifications to you as a trader are manifold. The first consequence of instant electronic access shows up in the cost of doing business. Back in 1980, a round turn commission for one bond futures contract was routinely in the range of $200. Now the same trade will cost you about two bucks. That means you can do a hundred times as many trades for the same net cost. This is exactly what has happened: Volume on the futures exchanges has exploded. New volume records are set practically every month, and why not? Every month competition for your business continues to drive costs lower.

But lower transaction costs do not benefit all traders equally. If the only thing you care about is getting in and out of the market as efficiently as possible, to you, interaction is simply interference, and the less of it the better. However, for other traders, one of the adverse consequences of lower cost is less service. That $200 used to buy a lot of feedback. Every human link in the trading chain between you and the pit had a unique perspective on the order flow, and each story was yours for the asking. You were entitled to talk to anyone who got paid for handling any part of your order.

In fact, one of the outcomes of better access is that the entire responsibility for every aspect of the trading process has been shifted directly onto you. The broker you used to deal with was in most cases a highly trained professional with a whole series of registrations and associations on his or her resume. Now you have to supply that depth of experience yourself. And experience in this arena cannot be discounted—it usually cannot be bought cheaply.

To reduce the impact of this experience deficit, there are several approaches you might take. Let's look at three. One approach would be simply to take advantage of the current historically low commissions and trade more. Another approach would be to join an online trading chat room. Still another would be to take on a trading partner.

The first approach, in which you simply trade more—a lot more, perhaps—is one in which it might be said that you attempt to force-feed your experience. It works for geese—why not for you? The reason force-feeding works for geese is that their diets have been worked out in advance by knowledgeable, if not overly sympathetic, animal husbandmen. As a trader, you are not simply stuffing yourself with trades. Although it is true that you want to devour as many good trades as possible, you need to have an idea of what a good trade looks like. In this approach, the possibility of many trials also implies the likelihood of many errors, and with the leverage that exists in the futures markets, it takes very few of the wrong kind of errors to thwart the whole process.

Online trading chat rooms have become very popular venues for both novice traders and experienced pit traders who might be transitioning to the e-markets. If you choose (for a fee), you will be permitted to see screen captures of the computer monitors of various traders in the room.

The third approach—taking on a trading partner—is the chosen route of many experienced traders. All of us who have traded for a livelihood bring a significant backlog of trading successes as well as failures (otherwise known as experience) into the mix. To many traders, even the idea of taking on a partner may seem impossible. After all, traders are a notoriously independent breed, often so guarded about our trading secrets that we are regarded widely as near-paranoid personality types. How does one partner up with that? You must choose a partner who has a strength different from yours. For example, if you are unfazed by catastrophe, you might choose as a partner someone who has a strong background in risk management.

Whatever approach you choose, the one most important step you *should* take is to pay for some trading education. This education should come before and underlie whatever additional steps you may take. If you are a novice, either a moderated chat room or a direct one-on-one tutorial is a good bet. If you are an experienced floor trader who is transitioning to the screen, some education in spreadsheet technique probably is in order.

Trick 4

Save $5,000 on Investment Advice

Minimum Activity	0	1	2	3	4	5	6	7	8	Maximum Activity

Why someone would pay $5,000 for investment advice is beyond comprehension. Do you really think a group of guys writing clever advertising copy are more knowledgeable than your brokers?

The truth of the matter is that I've worked at such firms. I admire their copywriting skills, but they are no more accurate at predicting the future than anyone else. However, I do enjoy their histrionics. Why so many are located in Florida still puzzles me.

Do the math.

If you can get 1,000 individuals to send you $5,000 each for your "nonguaranteed" advice, you have quite a business. Here's the real deal: Many of these firms talk you into buying options on "interest rates," "gold stocks," and "Canadian energy trusts."

For $5,000 you can take an investment course at a top-tier school such as Harvard, Yale, or the University of Chicago.

Here's what you should do:

1. Call your broker and ask about these hot newsletter traders.
2. Type the investment idea into any search engine, such as Google. For example, I typed in "Interest Rate Options" and eventually found the Chicago Options Exchange.
3. Remember, unless these advice services can show you a three-year track record, you might as well go fishing with a rifle. Aim at the water, pull the trigger, and pray you hit a fish.

If you want objective advice, seek out a fee-for-service financial planner. Or you could just get a financial magazine with a good reputation. Note the following table of stock picks.

In December 2004, *Fortune* magazine assembled the top gurus of the nation and predicted which stocks would be winners in 2005.

Company	Symbol	2004 Price, $	Price on March 14, 2006, $
Altria	MO	58.85	74.46
Ameren Corp.	AEE	48.36	50.68
Berkshire Hathaway	BRKB	2,802	2,981
ChevronTexaco	CVX	52.78	56.35
Citigroup	C	46.44	47.18
Covance	CVD	38.96	58.86
Electronic Arts	ERTS	52.46	52.94
Forest City Enterprises	FCEA	54.50	43.26
Freddie Mac	FRE	68.67	63.82
Heineken ADR	HINKY	32.45	32.25
Interpublic	IPG	12.88	10.03
Journal Register	JRC	18.50	12.94
Lloyds TSB ADR	LYG	33.43	38.12
Royal Dutch Petroleum ADR	RD	56.54	62.60
Tupperware	TUP	19.08	20.28
Turkish Investment Fund	TKF	13.00	26.96
Washington Mutual	WM	40.68	43.54
Wyeth	WYE	40.83	49.08

Trick 5

Always Read the Fine Print

Minimum Activity 0 1 2 3 4 5 6 7 8 Maximum Activity

I receive a newsletter from a software trading company. Read the following:

> Dear Trader:
> I'd like to introduce you to an amazing software program that makes child's play out of mastering stocks. But don't take my word for it. Just take a moment to meet Joey Johnson.

At 12 years of age, in his soccer shorts, Joey isn't your average Wall Street investor. But neither are his *triple-digit profits*. Joey began trading stocks just after his twelfth birthday, when his parents finally said he was old enough.

In his first six months, Joey's portfolio was *up 355 percent.*

How does a 12-year old generate triple-digit gains that would be the envy of almost any investor? Joey's secret is BidWiz, a user-friendly software program that tracks the supply and demand of individual stocks and graphically captures the stock's movement.

Dad's portfolio went up 500-plus percent

Joey has taken his "BidWiztrading" to heart—and to the bank. His mom and dad also use BidWiz and introduced him to the software. His mom, Treva, says, "My average over the last 26 trades has been a 12 to 13 percent gain." Joey's dad, Bob, adds that with

BidWiz, "Over the last 2½ years, I've probably increased my asset (base) over 500 or 600 percent."

"It saved our retirement account."

Now for the fine print

> BidWiz is a trademark of Wiggit Solutions, LLP. BidWiz is an analytical tool only and does not predict price trends. Testimonials included may not represent typical results. Unique experiences and past performances do not guarantee future results. Trading stocks involves substantial risk of loss. The purchase of, sale of, or giving advice regarding a stock can only be performed by a licensed Broker/Dealer or registered Investment Advisor. Wiggit Solutions, LLP and its owners, employees, and affiliates do not give investment advice, and none of them is a licensed Broker/Dealer or Registered Investment Advisor. Wigget Solutions, LLP encourages consultation with a licensed representative prior to making any particular investment or using any investment strategy.

This is what it actually states:

BidWiz is a trademark of Wiggit Solutions, LLP. BidWiz is an analytical tool only and does not predict price trends. Testimonials included may not represent typical results. Unique experiences and past performances do not guarantee future results. Trading stocks involve a substantial risk of loss. The purchase of, sale of, or giving advice regarding a stock can only be performed by a licensed broker-dealer or registered investment advisor. Wiggit Solutions, LLP, and its owners, employees, and affiliates do not give investment advice, and none of them is a licensed broker-dealer or registered investment advisor. Wigget Solutions, LLP, encourages consultation with a licensed representative prior to making any particular investment or using any investment strategy.

Trick 6

Minimizing Short-Term Trading Risk: Stocks or Futures?

Minimum									Maximum
Activity	0	1	2	3	4	5	6	7	8 Activity

By Cyril V. Smith, private futures trader

All market participants seek a level of risk that matches their comfort level in relation to their anticipated returns. Many people automatically assume that for short-term trading their risk will be lower with stocks as opposed to futures. That is not necessarily the case. Risk normally is measured by volatility of returns, and there are compelling reasons to believe that a futures trading portfolio may have less volatility than does one devoted to stocks.

Let's assume that a stock trading portfolio is limited to blue chips to minimize volatility. We certainly don't want the 13 percent one-day plunge that Google took recently. But even if we limit the stock universe to the bluest of the blue chips, we find that 10 percent one-day swings *such as Microsoft's recent 11* percent *drop* are not uncommon. By contrast, 10 percent one-day swings are practically unknown in broadly traded liquid futures markets such as T-bonds, crude oil, the major currencies, and corn. In some cases daily limits restrict moves, but even without them it is hard to find daily swings over 3 percent. When such moves do occur, there is often ample reason to think the market will be exceptionally volatile, such as the market for crude oil during a major Gulf Coast hurricane or a Mideast crisis.

I believe the reason for the greater intraday volatility of stocks is the lack of full information on the part of the investing public, even

17

in the case of industry leaders. IBM or Intel can always have an earnings surprise; Microsoft can change its business strategy. Real surprises, however, are few and far between in widely traded futures. What the Federal Reserve or OPEC is planning is widely known, and although the day-to-day implementation of those plans causes fluctuations in the market, it normally does not lead to excessive intraday volatility.

At this point the reader probably is thinking that with stock margins at 50 percent, a 10 percent adverse swing is easy to absorb. Futures margins, by contrast, are in the range of 2 to 3 percent, and so a 3 percent adverse swing would wipe out an account (if the position was invested to the margin limit). However, futures traders do not invest at the margin limit; those who do that do not remain futures traders for long. A good rule of thumb is to limit risk on a particular trade to 3 percent of equity. I always assume that risk is at least equal to margin, and so a $100,000 portfolio would trade just two T-bond contracts with a value of approximately $200,000 and a current margin requirement of $1,350. In short, by managing risk you can trade futures and reduce your exposure to volatility.

There is a second major advantage to futures: It is easier to construct a diversified noncorrelated portfolio. There is a large correlation between the movement of stocks, particularly blue chip stocks, and that of the market as a whole. A $100,000 stock trading portfolio, even one invested at the margin limit in a dozen stocks, has a substantial exposure to general market risk. In contrast, a $100,000 futures portfolio trading contract with positions of $3,000 worth of margin for T-bonds, crude oil, Eurocurrency, and corn simultaneously has nowhere near that correlation of that stock portfolio. A diversified noncorrelated portfolio in and of itself will reduce the volatility of returns. This phenomenon often is referred to as the financial world's only free lunch. Diversification of this degree is, I believe, far more easy to achieve with futures.

Trick 7

Spiders, Diamonds, and Qubes, Oh My!

Minimum  Maximum
Activity 0 1 2 3 4 5 6 7 8 Activity

If you plan to become an active trader, you must know how these products work.

- *Spiders (SPDRs)* track the Standard & Poor's (S&P) midcap index as well as sectors such as energy, financial services, and technology.

- Diamonds track the Dow Jones Industrial Average.

- Qubes track the Nasdaq 100 Composite stocks. The name is a play on words, since the ticker symbol is QQQ.

- Holdrs. These Merrill Lynch exchange traded funds (ETFs) track sectors such as pharmaceuticals and biotechnology and market indexes such as the Russell 2000.

- iShares. From Barclays Global Investors, iShares offer the largest number of ETFs, covering every major U.S. and foreign stock market index.

- StreetTracks, from State Street Global Advisors, cover the Dow Jones and Morgan Stanley indexes.

This is why you should have two brokerage firms. The big full-service one will take you step by step through the derivatives jungle.

Trick 8

Pump Up the Volume with Excel

Minimum Activity 0 1 2 3 4 5 6 7 8 Maximum Activity

By Barrett Fiske, full-time trader

As recently as the 1999 revised edition of Murphy's *Technical Analysis of the Financial Markets,* we were told the following about volume:

> [V]olume reporting in the stock market is much more useful than in the futures markets. Stock volume is reported immediately, while it is reported a day later for futures.

Electronic futures trading has come a long way in the last five years. Every trick in the volume book that any long- or short-term stock trader has tried is now available to online intraday futures traders. And it gets better: The use of volume in a spreadsheet format allows an online trader to mimic most of the pit experience of a floor trader.

Let's take a quick step back to set the scene.

The high failure rate experienced by formerly successful floor traders when they attempt to transition to screen-based trading is well documented. The reason for it is obvious to all: Something is getting lost in translation. The solution is simple in concept but anything but simple in execution: The pit experience must be reproduced in a virtual environment.

Traders have experimented with a variety of methods to achieve an acceptable simulation. One trading group's solution was to put phone clerks in the pit. A clerk's job is to quote the market all session long: Who's buying? Who's selling? How much? Are the locals going with the trade or attempting to turn it back? This is information that a seasoned pit trader takes in at a glance. In fact, there are now clerk groups that sell subscription-based live pit quoting.

Another trading group's attempt at a solution took a slightly different tack. Pit traders are a notoriously iconoclastic lot, and rather than filter the action through the perceptions of an unknown clerk, some traders have elected simply to watch the pit on closed-circuit television while listening to the action through headphones.

Both of these solutions represent an attempt to do the same thing: measure the buying or selling pressure on each price tick. Fortunately, this is an operation Excel can manage for you very easily. Unfortunately, however, it's not an operation that is at all easy to program. Further complicating matters is the fact that it requires several macros, none of which are in Excel's standard library of macros. You will need a little bit of custom programming. (I'm reminded of a line from *A League of Their Own*. Tom Hanks's character says about baseball, "It's supposed to be hard. If it wasn't hard, everyone would do it. The hard is what makes it great.")

I can't stress enough how important it is to have some measure of volume incorporated into your analysis. I will give you a brief description of what the macro does. You should be able to take this description to an expert Excel programmer and he or she will incorporate it into your spreadsheet. (If you don't know anyone who can do this for you, contact the author and he will refer you.)

Price/Volume Pressure

Create a link to the current price in cell A1. Every minute, have the macro direct the current price to drop down one row. Subtract the price in that row from the price in the previous row. This will give you the change for the last minute.

In cell B1, open a link to volume. Then, in cell C1, multiply the change for the last minute times the volume for that minute. The result will represent the price/volume (P/V) pressure for that minute. Have this cell drop down a row every minute and you can keep a running track of the pressure on every price change during the trading day.

Once you have this basic information, you can use it in a number of ways. For example, you may sum the most recent 10 minutes of P/V pressure and compare it to the P/V pressure of the previous 10 minutes.

According to the standard interpretation of price and volume, an increase in price accompanied by high volume denotes a much stronger market than does a similar price increase accompanied by average volume.

All you need is a little—well, more than a little—Excel programming, and you can go a long ways toward replicating a critically important piece of information that was formerly the sole and private purview of floor traders. In short, do they take customer service seriously or keep saying, "Please hold. Your call is important to us."

Trick 9

Pretend You're a Customer

Minimum ▮▮▮▮ •• Maximum
Activity 0   1   2   3   4   5   6   7   8 Activity

Before you purchase software, a computer, or any type of product, pretend you're already a customer and call the "customer service" department. Sounds simple, right? How many menus are there to go through, and after that how long are you placed on hold? Can you understand what they are saying? Is there an 800 number?

Now do the same thing with an online broker you're thinking of using. What's that? They don't answer the phone? But they will suggest that you use their gang of full-service brokers who aren't allowed to trade for their own accounts but will gladly give trading tips.

If you are on a cell phone, you will use 10 to 20 minutes of phone time. If you have a problem, you'd better bring a battery pack.

Tip 1

Pin Drop

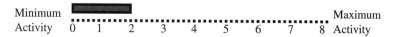

Minimum Activity   0   1   2   3   4   5   6   7   8   Maximum Activity

What Do You Do When the Sky Is Falling?

Chicken Little was hit on the head by an object that fell from the sky. With that event, he believed the sky was falling. He proclaimed to the world, "The sky is falling! The sky is falling!" Then, in the movie trailer, the question is, "What would you do if the sky was falling?" Hmm. I know. Sell the sky.

Tip 2

No Cash? Consider a Trading Arcade, Algorithmic Trading Firm, or FX Group

Minimum Activity  Maximum Activity

0   1   2   3   4   5   6   7   8

You can get paid to trade. There are trading arcades and algorithmic trading firms that are always looking for bright traders. In fact, the entire industry is in its incipiency.

Be sure to visit the Web site of an arcade before you contact anyone by phone or e-mail. The list below is not complete, and there are arcades opening all the time. In fact, there are groups all over the planet. Always ask, "Are any other firms hiring?" Never leave a job interview without a reference.

Software vendors are also great sources for knowing which firms are hiring people. Read the financial press. Notice who is quoted and what firm these people represent. E-mail these contacts or visit the Web site. Many of these firms are looking for traders.

To really stand out, learn a front-end trading system. This is high-stress active trading. Good luck. You'll need it.

Trading Arcades and Proprietary Trading Houses

Note: This is a starting point only.

ALTEA TRADING COMPANY LLC

One North Wacker Drive, Suite 777
Chicago, IL 60606
Phone: 312-214-0700
www.alteatrading@alteatrading.com

THE ARCHELON GROUP

200 S. Wacker, 24th Floor
Chicago, IL 60606
Phone: 312-461-0300
Fax: 312-461-9536
Phone: 312-788-6380
www.archelongroup.com

CONSOLIDATED TRADING LLC

Whitney Lamberson
440 S. LaSalle, Suite 3400
Chicago, IL 60605
Phone: 312 260-5428
www.wlamberson@consolidatedtrading.com

DE TRADING CORP. / INTERNATIONAL TRADING GROUP

Loren H. Newman
DE Trading Corp.
Phone: 847-724-3215
www.trader520@detrading.com

DRW TRADING GROUP

10 S. Riverside Plaza, 21st Floor
Chicago, IL 60606

Phone: 312-542-1000
www.hr@drwtrading.com

FUSIONARY TRADING
30 S. Wacker Drive, Suite 1420
Chicago, IL 60606
www.fusionarytrading.com

GATOR TRADING PARTNERS, LLC
Gator Trading Partners, LLC
V.P. Portfolio Management
175 W. Jackson, Suite 420
Chicago, IL 60604
www.mtpaul@gsb.uchicago.edu

GENEVA TRADING
980 N. Michigan Ave., Suite 1710
Chicago, IL 60611
312-587-7000 x 100 General Enquiry
www.geneva-trading.com
jobs@geneva-trading.com

GETCO, LLC
141 W. Jackson Blvd., Suite 210
Chicago, IL 60604
312-242-4600
www.akrasowska@getcollc.com

GHCO (GOLDENBERG, HEHMEYER & CO.)
John DeMartino
141 W. Jackson Ave., Suite 1701A
Chicago, IL 60604
Phone: 312-356-6040
www.ghco.com

HARRISON TRADING GROUP, LLC
601 S. LaSalle St., Suite 200
Chicago, IL 60605
Phone: 312-327-4000
Fax: 312-638-7088
www.Hr@harrisontradinggroup.com

KC-CO II, LLC
10 S. LaSalle Street, Suite 2300
Chicago, IL 60603
Phone: 312-762-2800
www.Employment2004@kcco.com

MARQUETTE PARTNERS LP
801 West Adams (corner of Adams and Halsted), Suite 500
Chicago, IL 60607
Phone: 312-224-2400
Fax: 312-224-2402
www.resumes@mqplp.com

RHO TRADING SECURITIES, LLC
Human Resources: Mindy Wilson,
Rho Trading Securities, LLC
Direct Phone: 312-362-4986
Main Phone: 312-362-4990
Fax: 312-873-4315
www.mindy@rhotrading.com

SAXON FINANCIALS LIMITED
15-25 Artillery Lane
London, E1 7LP, UK
Phone: +44 20 7247 9000
Fax: +44 20 7247 9000
www.info@saxonfinancials.com

SMW TRADING COMPANY, INC

141 W. Jackson Blvd., Suite 380
Chicago, IL 60604
Phone: 312-913-6100
Fax: 312-663-1317
www.smwtrading.com

TRANSMARKET GROUP, LLC

141 W. Jackson Blvd., Suite 1930
Chicago, IL 60604
Phone: 312-663-4900
Fax: 312-663-4906
www.collegerecruiting@tmgchicago.com
www.transmarketgroup.com

TRINITY CAPITAL MARKETS, LLC

www.cmcnulty@thetrinitygroup.net

UNIVERSITY OF TRADING

Note: Mickey Hoffman is an instructor at the Chicago
   Mercantile Exchange. He receives high marks from his
   students.
Dr. Michael K. "Mickey" Hoffman
312-334-5882
www.uot@earthlink.net
www.universityoftrading.com

THE WESCOTT GROUP

30 S. Wacker Drive, Suite1108
Chicago, IL 60606

WOLVERINE TRADING, LLC

www.contactus@wolve.com
Focus in on stock options. One of my foreign interns is now a
   trader there and now buys me dinner. But he won't hire me.

Algorithmic Trading Directory

Company Name	Contact Information	Description of Services
Aegis Software Inc.	212-651-9465 www.aegisoft.com	Front-end trading system
BNY Brokerage	212-468-7812 800-828-5454 x 7812 www.bny.com	Services trading platform; offers a comprehensive set of standardized and customized trading tools, rules, and algorithms
BofA	212-847-6861 www.bofasecurities.com/ets	Electronic trading system platform provides institutions with automated access to liquidity systems and venues; supports stocks, blocks, and direct-market-access programs
Citigroup Global Capital Markets	800-541-9398 www.citigroup.com	Offers innovative, market-leading algorithmic trading strategies
Credit Suisse First Boston	CSFB AES Trading Desk 212-325-5300 www.csfb.com	Automated trading strategies, tools, and analytics for global equity trading
Electronic Specialist LLC	Scott Kurland 212-485-5127 www.fastesp.com	Clients can trade anonymously with more than 30 algorithms
FlexTrade Systems Inc.	516-627-8993 x 236 www.sales@flextrade.com www.flextrade.com	Global trading and order management system

(Continued)

Company Name	Contact Information	Description of Services
Goldman, Sachs & Co.	www.goldmansachs. com	Provides clients with access to proprietary and pre- and posttrade analytics
Instinet, LLC	212-310-9500 www.instinet.com	Offers a comprehensive suite of algorithmic strategies with access to global equity markets
ITG Inc.	www.itginc.com	ITG's Smart Servers provide a comprehensive suite of trading algorithms designed to meet multiple benchmarks and automate trading tactics to enhance performance
JPMorgan Securities	www.jpmorgan.com	Enables clients to execute stock orders electronically according to sophisticated algorithms that help minimize market impact
Lehman Brothers	www.lehmanlive.com	LMX is Lehman Brothers' suite of model-driven order execution strategies operating in 18 countries
Merril Lynch	212-449-6090 www.mix.ml.com	ML X-ACT is a performance-driven automated trading platform

Miletus Trading	800-450-7161 www.miletustrading.com	Miletus Trading, LLC, is a quantities broker-dealer specializing in algorithmic-based automated trade execution
Morgan Stanley, Inc.	212-761-8881 www.morganstanley.com	The Benchmark Execution Strategies (BXS) are designed to manage the relationship between impact and market risk dynamically
Orc Software	646-435-2062 ext. 222 www.orcsoftware.com	Orc Liquidator was designed for cross-market arbitrage; developed as a black-box trading system
Portware	212-425-5233 www.portware.com	The global trade-execution-management platform for multiasset baskets
Sanford C. Bernstein	212-823-2896 www.sanfordbernstein.com	Offers a comprehensive set of tools that enable buy-side traders to improve their performance and consistency
TradeTrek Securities, LLC	973-456-7008 www.tradetrek.com www.algorithmictrading.com	Offers an extensive menu of next-generation algorithms
UNX, Inc.	818-333-3300 www.unx.com	An institutionally focused agency brokerage firm that offers proprietary electronic trading capabilities

33

Foreign Exchange Multidealer Directory

State Street Corp.	617-644-2526 www.globalink.com	FX Connect is a multibank foreign exchange trading network that provides secure real-time trade execution with multiple counterparties 24 hours a day
360 Treasury Systems AG	www.360t.com	TEX Multidealer Trading System, 360t's globally accessible cross-product multibank portal, offers a single window of professional market access, corporate treasuries, institutionals, buy-side banks, and public sector trade FX, MM, and other frequently used financial instruments with market makers of their choice on a Web-based execution platform
Chicago Mercantile Exchange (CME)	312-930-1000 www.cme.com	The Chicago Mercantile Exchange's electronic trading platform for foreign exchange and all CME products; check the CME Web site for jobs

Lava Trading Inc.

David Ogg 212-609-0100
www.lavafx.com
www.lavatrading.com

The LavaFX product suite, built on Lava's proprietary technology core, provides a premier offering in electronic foreign exchange trading that is transforming the FX's central limit order book; provides live dealable prices, full price transparency and depth of book, and the ability to place bids and offers, together with Lava's sophisticated order types

Currenex Inc.

877-939-8723
www.currenex.com

A comprehensive suite of FX and money markets trading tools for the buy and sell sides; offers executable streaming prices, request for streams, benchmark trading, and complete prime brokerage functionality with fully integrated pre- and posttrade processing services

Prestidigitation 1

Humility Is Better than Hubris

| Minimum | | | | | | | | | Maximum |
| Activity | 0 | 1 | 2 | 3 | 4 | 5 | 6 | 7 | 8 | Activity |

After the United States entered World War I, there was widespread hatred of all things German. Many schools stopped teaching the German language. Sauerkraut, a German dish made from cabbage, was renamed liberty cabbage. Hamburgers, named after a city in Germany, were renamed liberty sausage. After 9/11, French fries were renamed freedom fries.

Getting involved in world events, especially emotionally involved, will result in your becoming part of the crowd, the mob, and the public. Not good.

What's Been Your Most Humbling Experience?

"Trading. You develop a sense of humility in regard to your guesses about the market, and humility is a very important thing when it comes to trading in financial markets. You pay your price up front. You have good days and bad days, and the bad days remind you that you're not smarter than the market. You need to stick to what you know from a trading standpoint." Thomas Pickett, president and CEO of Incapital Holdings LLC.

Freakonomics

Steven Levitt isn't likely to tell you whether the stock market will go up or the economy will shrink. Nobody can predict the market, so if your name is Sy Nercom, grin and accept it. But ask him why drug dealers live with their moms, why crime rates *really* dropped in the last decade, or what makes a good parent, and he'll not only tell you the answer but show you the data to back it up. In *Freakonomics*, Levitt and coauthor Stephen Dubner use Levitt's research to explore how people get what they want, especially when other people want the same thing. Written for a general audience, the book uncovers the economics in everyday life, from how school-teachers cheat and real estate agents act like the Ku Klux Klan to how a child's name affects his or her chances for success. (Levitt argues that that it's not the name but the child's socioeconomic background, sometimes reflected in the name, that is determinant.)

When the stock market crashed in 1987, the temperature outside the Chicago Board of Trade was 52°F. Keep that in mind every time the temperature is 52°F.

And remember that when you rearrange the letters in *slot machines* it becomes "cash lost in me."

Tip 3

If You Can't Remember 1929, Reflect on September 11

Minimum
Activity  Maximum
Activity

0   1   2   3   4   5   6   7   8

The following reflection was given to me by a hedge fund trader:

> The first thing that came to mind the morning of September 11, 2001 was: *Our country is under attack!* I was not feeling well that Monday morning and decided to stay home with my wife and boys. It had been a hectic two weeks for my trading, and a long weekend was in order. I showered and was getting ready for a relaxing day.
>
> As a trader, I was still focusing on the markets and was brushing up on the current news on CNBC. As I watched *Squawk Box*, Mark Haines cut to a report that the World Trade Center had been hit by an airplane. I didn't think much of it—an accident—and went along with my business.
>
> While continuing to watch, I witnessed on live television the second plane hitting the other tower. *Immediately*, I thought back to the sixth grade. I was sick when the space shuttle *Challenger* blew up on January 28, 1986. As I watched the space shuttle being engulfed in flames, I felt totally helpless and vulnerable, being a 12-year-old.
>
> *Vulnerable* is exactly how I felt on September 11, 2001, only now I have a wife and two children to take care of. My nonemotional approach and discipline toward the markets went out the window when I heard that the Pentagon had been hit. I did not

care about the *Trade*. I needed to be strong and make sure they were safe.

Vulnerable is where the market is currently. As of midday October 30, 2001, the Dow has lost 440 points in two days. The financial markets are extremely susceptible to news, and I don't feel comfortable in a long only position, I feel slightly more confident in the short side but am ready to change my position at the drop of a dime.

This incident has changed the way investors and traders approach the market. The week before the tragedy, I began trading a statistical arbitrage strategy in which I trade highly correlated equities. I am short one equity, long another. It has been successful for me in a couple of ways. First, I have been making money every day, hitting singles and doubles each time at bat. Second, I feel much more comfortable with a "hedged" position in which I can withstand any type of news.

This approach allows me to book a nice profit or limit my losses. I have also been trading a momentum strategy in the e-mini Nasdaq and S&P. I feel much more at ease trading a momentum strategy in stock index futures in which I can con-centrate on news in a broader sense. I can limit my losses to a single tick or two. You never know when an anthrax scare will hit, a new terrorist act will occur, or the war in Afghanistan will end.

All publications prior to September 11, 2001, are obsolete. Our society was satisfied with the illusion of security until terrorism once again hit our shores. The manner in which we approach the market and specific trades will change.

My comment follows:

The market runs on psychology. People buy because they expect prices to go up. No amount of press coverage or hype can influence consumer psychology.

Negative news can influence the markets in seconds. Your portfolio can plunge 50 percent or more. You should always have a portion of your portfolio in government securities. Why? Because in a financial crisis, there will be a flight to quality. If you trade options, never sell calls or puts over a weekend.

Prestidigitation 2

Is Security a Problem?

Minimum  Maximum
Activity 0   1   2   3   4   5   6   7   8 Activity

The question on everyone's lips is, What is behind the other investment door? Why risk financial death when there is a virtual plethora of investment options?

When I taught securities analysis, one assignment stated: Given various assumptions regarding risk and return objectives and certain parameters, conduct an evaluation of the investment environment and recommend a suitable overall investment strategy. Well, there is a simple way of doing that. Merely call or e-mail your broker.

The following list of Web sites is currently formidable. We suggest you choose two brokers and two Web sites for research. As you scan a Web site, you will design an industry. We seldom do research on companies that are making us money. We usually want to find out why only when we are "losing."

List of Full-service Firms and Web Sites

A.G. Edwards
http://www.agedwards.com/

Bank of America
http://www.bankofamerica.com/

Charles Schwab
http://www.charlesschwab.com

Dean Witter/Morgan Stanley
http://www.deanwitter.com/

Fidelity
https://www.fidelity.com/

J.P. Morgan
http://www.jpmorganchase.com/

LPL Financial Services
http://www.lpl.com/html/index.html

Merrill Lynch
http://www.ml.com/

Prudential Financial
http://www.prudential.com/

TD Waterhouse
http://www.tdwaterhouse.com/home.asp

Investment Information

10K Wizard: a great site for building a financial toolbox
http://www.10kwizard.com

Biospace: for Biotech Companies
http://www.biospace.com

CBS MarketWatch: a news and information service
http://cbs.marketwatch.com

Financial Times: excellent reporting
http://news.ft.com/home/us

FleetKids: filled with online money gurus
http://www.fleetkids.com

Hoover's Online: a great research tool
http://www.hoovers.com

Investopedia: tutorials and an investing encyclopedia
http://www.investopedia.com

Investor's Business Daily: focuses on issues and rules for traders
http://www.investors.com

Kiplinger: provides a perspective on a daily basis
http://kiplinger.com

Marketocracy: obtains alerts on buying
http://marketrocracy.com

Motley Fool: cute and informative
http://fool.com

Prophet.net: get the seven-day trial
http://www.profet.net

Reuters Investor: has a solid reputation for great
    reporting
http://www.investor.reuters.com

RiskGrades: will tell you how risky your stock is
http://riskgrades.com

ValueEngine.com: a great way to value your stocks
http://www.valueengine.com

Wall Street City: helps you custom design your own
    searches
http://wallstreetcity.com

Mutual Fund Selection

Mutual Fund Investor: finds funds that cost less than $50
http://www.mfea.com

Mutual Funds

Brill's Mutual Funds Interactive
http://www.brill.com/features.html

Dreyfus Corporation
http://www.dreyfus.com

Janus Funds
http://www.janus.com

ProFunds: Continuously top-rated funds
http://www.profunds.com

Online Trading

American Express Financial Direct
http://www.americanexpress.com/direct

Ameritrade
http://www.ameritrade.com

E*Trade
http://www.etrade.com

FOLIOn
http://wwwfolion.com

HARRISdirect
http://harrisdirect.com

iDS Finance
http://wwwidsfinance.com

Morgan Stanley
http://morganstanley.com

Scottrade
http://www.scottrade.com

Tip 4

Don't Count on Beginner's Luck

By Larry Schneider

*Larry Schneider has taught many traders. He is an instructor
at the Chicago Mercantile Exchange. He can be reached at
the Zaner Group in Chicago, where he is currently director
of sales and marketing.*

Minimum Activity   0   1   2   3   4   5   6   7   8   Maximum Activity

For over 30 years I've observed traders: the dilettantes and the serious students of the markets, the successful and the unsuccessful, and, most interesting, the highfliers who flame out too soon.

What have I learned?

If you are a new trader, regardless of your net worth or the size of your risk capital, two lessons stand out. First, give serious consideration to your "pain threshold." This is the point at which you will admit, "I am wrong, the market is right, and no one wins by being overly stubborn." The pain threshold is the loss level at which you will close out open positions, cancel resting good-till-cancelled orders, and close your futures account. I know this sounds negative, but it is a factor in one's personal trading plan that must be considered. Also, it is a level that must be decided on before you begin trading. It is always far easier to consider this number coldly and rationally when there is no money on the table. Remember, no one's funds are unlimited.

46

Many years ago, I worked for a very successful trader. One day he showed me his statement and pointed out that while he was long or short about 15 different contracts, the position in each commodity was never larger than a 3-lot. Knowing how successful he was, I asked him why he wasn't holding 2 or even 20 contracts per commodity. Surely if he could make x points on a 1-lot, he would reap 10 times that amount on a 10-lot. His answer was as follows. He said that if he traded larger than a 3-lot, he would begin to lose all perspective. He would no longer focus on the potential of, say, corn moving from $2.00 to $2.50 but instead would be too hung up on the absolute amount of money he was making (or losing!) on a position of 10 corn contracts. He said, "Better to be right 80 percent of the time with 1-lots than have your equity be swinging wildly and ultimately wind up on the losing side [study the price, not the money]." Conversely, I recall a client of a major wire house I once worked for who started out small and seemingly never was on the wrong side of the market. He focused on currencies, and his quick success with 5-and 10-contract positions soon saw him holding very large positions. On one fateful day that was characterized by whipsaw rallies and declines, this trader went from long 200, to short 200, back to long 200, and finally out. Each loss was larger than the previous one, and in one trading session he gave back all the profits he had accumulated, profits that allowed him to have the margin to hold 200 contracts. The lesson: The fact that you have the capital to support 200 contracts in a single commodity does not necessarily mean you should do so.

Avoiding errors won't make you money, but it will prevent you from losing money needlessly.

No one likes to lose money, but serious traders never take their losses personally. It's always a matter of "The market was right, and I was wrong. I'll take my losses early and wait for the next opportunity." But errors are another story. An error does not necessarily mean a mistake that costs you money; an error is an action you made without intending to. It just seems that errors always cost you money. Here is my list of the most common errors traders make.

1. Thinking like a stock trader and liquidating a short position with a sell order. Since most stock traders enter the market with a buy order, they naturally liquidate the position with a sell order. But futures traders are equally comfortable trading from the short side, and that means liquidating a short position with a buy order. (Back in the days before screen trading, when clients had to call orders directly to the brokerage firm, it was not uncommon to have a client call and say: "Buy me short" or "Sell my shorts." Pity the confused clerk or broker who had to interpret that kind of misplaced order.)

2. Forgetting about good-till-canceled orders. More frequently than you'd believe, clients wind up with a trade they never wanted because they completely forget about a good-till-canceled order they entered months back. This can be especially dangerous when one is approaching the delivery month, when many contracts remove the daily limits and intraday price swings get larger than usual. That good-till-canceled soybean order that was $1.50 away from the market can get filled before you know it, and suddenly you have a position you never knew you had.

3. Confusing eurodollars with eurocurrency. Eurodollar Time Deposit futures is a 90-day interest rate contract. Its nickname is "euro." The EuroFX is a currency contract based on the currency of the European Monetary Union. Its nickname is "euro" too. Broadly speaking, eurodollar futures is more of an institutional market. That's why I always get suspicious when retail clients tell me they want to go long or short eurodollars. More times than not, they mean EuroFX currency futures.

4. Failing to check your statements each morning. Despite the current computerization of order entry, order matching, and reporting, mistakes get made. It is imperative that traders know that they and they alone are responsible for checking their statements each morning and immediately reporting a discrepancy to the brokerage firm. This can mean a trade that shows up by mistake, a confirmed trade that is missing, or a price different from what was confirmed previously. It is very difficult to go back to a firm several days after the fact and complain about a position.

5. Forgetting that the fact that the underlying commodity is the same doesn't make all futures contracts equal. Earlier this year, I called a broker to remind him that July silver's last trading day was just three days away and his client needed to close out his short position. The broker told me there had to be a mistake, because he had entered a spread order two weeks earlier in order to roll the short position from July to September. I took a look at both the client's position and the order that was placed and discovered that the broker had entered the spread to the Chicago Board of Trade (CBOT) despite the fact that the client had been short Comex silver. The result: short 5 July Comex silver, long 5 CBOT July silver, and short 5 CBOT September silver. Of course, a simple check of the client's statement by either the broker or the client the day after the July–September CBOT spread was entered would have caught the error, and we could have corrected it easily. But CBOT silver[1] is a lot less liquid than a Comex contract, and this illiquidity is far greater when there

---

[1] CBOT trades both a 1,000-ounce contract and a 5,000-ounce contract. The Comex is a 5,000-ounce contract.

is just three days before the contract's expiration. I had to work a limit order on the July CBOT silver, pricing it off the relatively active September Comex contract. As soon as I was able to sell July CBOT, I then had to enter a market order to buy July Comex. Although silver is silver, when it comes to 1,000 one-ounce bars sitting in a New York City bank depository, it's quite another matter to trade out of an expiring futures contract when the open interest is next to nothing.

A Common Mistake Made by Fledgling Options-on-Futures Traders

Too many novice options traders think they have "discovered" an investment secret no one else knows about. For many years I was the transaction futures product manager for Morgan Stanley DW Inc. Allow me to re-create a typical phone call I would have with a stockbroker and his or her client. Let me emphasize that these clients were characterized as high-net-worth individuals and that the decision to trade options on futures was theirs alone. The calls were all somewhat similar, so I'll use crude oil to illustrate my point. Typically, crude oil would have completed a significant advance, and these clients were looking to buy puts in anticipation of an impending break. The call would play out like this:

> Client: I believe crude is going to break in the next three weeks, and I want to buy puts.
> Me: Okay, let's look at current futures prices and option premiums to see what's out there. Near-term futures are trading at $61.50 a barrel, so let's look at a slightly out-of-money put

expiring in three weeks, per your outlook. Sixty-dollar puts are trading at $6.15[2] so if you buy them, you're actually stating a belief that you believe crude oil futures can decline from the current $61.50 to $53.85[2] in the next three weeks. Is this what you anticipate?

Client: No. I don't think the market will go below $55.00 a barrel.

Me: But you do realize that in buying a $60 put for $6.15 you need to have the underlying market fall to $53.85 by the option's expiration (in three weeks) just to break even? That's a drop of $7.65 a barrel from current prices. Anyone who buys this option right now is trading on the anticipation that crude can drop that far in just three weeks.

Client: No, I didn't realize that. I thought I could buy these puts for a whole lot less. Maybe this isn't such a good idea right now.

In truth, it wasn't a good idea. Novice traders fail to realize that options are priced very efficiently, and when you're looking at volatile markets, both puts and calls will be priced accordingly (translation, Expensive, or to use industry slang, "priced rich"). One must always calculate breakeven before leaping into an options trade.

---

[2] Crude oil is priced in terms of dollars and cents per barrel based on a 1,000-barrel contract. Breakeven for puts is strike price minus premium.

Tip 5

Action Point

The longer shelf life of facts and figures in the information age can provide considerable benefits when it comes to making important investment decisions. For the most part, it is relatively easy to access reams of data, news, and insights from online resources such as corporate Web sites, government data banks, and a variety of online information providers. The online resources include investment Web sites, such as the following:

http://finance.yahoo.com
http://moneycentral.msn.com
http://cbs.marketwatch.com
www.thestreet.com
www.fool.com;financial
www.bloomberg.com
www.wsj.com
www.investors.com

Then there are alternative news providers such as the following:

www.drudgereport.com
www.worldnetdaily.com

With these resources, individuals often can engage in the necessary "due diligence" in a matter of hours or days rather than weeks or months. Undoubtedly, this eliminates at least one excuse for not doing the requisite homework beforehand.

Tip 6

The Government Will Not Protect You

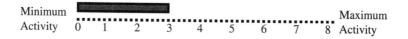

Minimum Activity 0 1 2 3 4 5 6 7 8 Maximum Activity

Back in December 1941, when the "War Department" knew that Bataan was a lost cause, the troops heard rumors that help was on the way. Even President Roosevelt said that "every vessel available" was en route to Luzon. In some ways he was right. Unfortunately, the troops could not hold out until 1944. In the end, 73,000 men were captured, and 37 percent of them died.

Certainly this is an extreme example and does take into account the desperate shape of our military in those bleak days. But this chapter in our history is worth remembering, because variations repeat themselves year after year.

Fast-forward to the present. The government does not insure stocks, mutual funds, and 401(k)s and deposits over $100,000. If your brokerage firm goes bust, you are out of luck. The government does not insure the New York Stock Exchange, the Chicago Board of Trade, or any other exchange.

If your company goes bankrupt as a result of fraud, well, too bad. In many of my seminars I tell people there is a torpedo that has your name on it. It is a financial torpedo that has the ability to rock your financial world. You have a choice: Put all your wealth on one ship or use a convoy.

Look what happened at Enron. Those people saw their hopes and dreams of a secure future evaporate. People who knew Social

Security would not be sufficient for retirement and planned for it *were wiped out*. Company loyalty is a thing of the past. A human resources department is a slick name for propaganda. An auditing firm or annual report means nothing. Figures don't lie, but liars can figure. Deregulation was supposed to get government off our backs so that public utilities, phone companies, and airlines could lower prices. Well, look at your bills. What happened to those savings? Just think: The airlines did not want to have a metal door installed on the planes because it cost too much. They were right. It indeed ended up costing Americans *too much*.

Tip 7

A Zebra in Lion Country

Minimum Activity  Maximum Activity

0 1 2 3 4 5 6 7 8

Investors are like zebras in lion country. I didn't say that, but I wish I had. That gem of a quote is the title of Ralph Wanger's book. Wanger believes that investors settle for meager pickings by sticking in the middle of the herd or seek richer rewards at the outer edge, where hungry lions lurk. That can be a very scary place. Wanger shows investors, whether they are investing in mutual funds or buying stocks on their own, how to achieve the right balance of safety and risk to survive and prosper in the investment jungle. Destined to become a classic in the field of investing, *A Zebra in Lion Country* is as entertaining as it is instructive.

Tip 8

Keep Your Eye on the Ball

By Jonathan Hoenig

Jonathan Hoenig is managing member at Capitalistpig Hedge Fund LLC (http://www.capitalistpig.com). He appears regularly on Fox News Channel and Smartmoney.com.

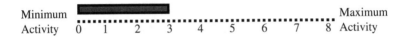

Minimum Activity								Maximum Activity
0	1	2	3	4	5	6	7	8

Some people won't miss an episode of *CSI* but have no idea what their 401(k) has done over the last six months. And there are those who bought Exxon after Hurricane Katrina and haven't looked at the stock since. They know who Lindsay Lohan is but couldn't tell you where the S&P 500 closed last week.

These people, many of them college-educated and extremely affluent, play the stock market the way you play the lottery: Buy a ticket and hope for the best. The market interests them only up to the point where they actually have to put in some effort. For such people, "buy and hold" has become "buy and blame." After all, it isn't *their* fault they lost money. It's the hedge funds', the analysts', or Ben Bernanke's fault.

Trading is first and foremost an exercise in *observation*. Despite the misconception that traders pull the trigger from bell to bell, you should spend most of your time watching, not making transactions. Like a chef, a traffic cop, or the plate-spinning guy on Ed Sullivan, good traders are able to observe a large volume of rapidly changing information. All the data needed to detect what's happening in the market can be found in the market itself, not in the heavens, the message boards, or the always-hedged analysis of well-paid pundits.

Although it seems obvious that a market participant should watch the market, you'd be surprised how many professional investors seem to do everything but that. Because of the popularity of index investing during the late 1990s, many investors stopped observing the market and started simply pitching its virtues. You ask them about the action, and they'll talk about the economy, politics, earnings, interest rates—everything under the sun *except* the price action. A money manager's job isn't to pontificate about the government or opine about the economy but to watch the markets. We're traders, not panelists on *Meet the Press*.

There is no shortage of indicators, reports, and data points to consider. And because of the sheer volume of statistics to consider, analysis can become paralysis very fast. But because you can't focus on everything, you've got to focus on what matters, and that's price—end of story.

I watch prices. Not the company's breakthrough product, insider selling, or the strong buy issued by the talking head who doesn't own a share. The price is what we trade, and so the price is what I watch.

To begin with, watch the stocks you own. As simplistic as it sounds, plenty of people don't know where their holdings are trading, let alone how they are trading relative to other securities. When the market was going straight up in the late 1990s, they couldn't take their eyes off the screen. Now I talk to plenty of "traders" who check their smoke detectors more often than they check their portfolios. Stocks are like your children. You need to keep tabs on them at all times.

So how does it open? If it's a New York Stock Exchange stock, what *time* does it open? Where does it trade midday, afternoon, and near the closing bell? Watch the volume. Watch how it responds to news and how it closes and trades in the aftermarket.

Next and perhaps most important, watch other names in the sector. The market isn't chaotic; it follows observable and established trends. And stocks are herd animals: They travel in packs. To that end, analyze the stock on its own merits and as a member of its industry or sector, along with that sector as a component of the overall market. Put together, these indicators give me an idea of what's happening in the sector better than Maria Bartiromo ever could.

Of course, nobody knows what's going to happen in the future. In a sense, we're all "dumb money." But the people who put in the most time in my opinion are slightly less dumb than the rest. Trading is less about anticipating what might happen than about understanding what's happening right here, right now. The best way to know that is to watch the market. That's what we trade. That's what counts.

Tip 9

Meet Captain Ron and Ship's Mate Stubby

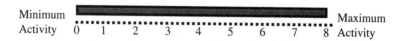

Minimum
Activity

0   1   2   3   4   5   6   7   8

Maximum
Activity

The following are actual notes written eight weeks before the Dow made its all-time high.

It was another chilly December night in Chicago. The year was 1999. It had been two months since we retired the 40-foot *Floating Prime* to its winter quarters in Racine, Wisconsin, and I was eager to meet my sailing buddies again.

We agreed to meet at La Vita, a quaint restaurant on Taylor Street in the Little Italy section of Chicago.

Captain Ron and Ship's Mate Stubby (don't ask me why they call him Stubby) arrived about 20 minutes late. I was expecting an apology, but Ron's first words were, "Guess what. My son made $25,000 today trading. He tried to short Yahoo! but eventually caught a short play in Coral."

Within a few years, euphoria turned to pessimism.

Our Generation X waiter, overhearing the conversation, said, "That's great. I trade too."

"Really," I replied, anxious to order.

"Yeah, I bought a stock called NTRL. Check it out." Well, the rest of the meal's conversation focused on the market and extrapolating market gains into the future. This can't be real, I thought as I drove home listening to a bunch of dot-com commercials.

When I finally arrived home that evening, I barely managed to catch the third ring of my telephone. "Hi, Mom. What's up?"

"Neal, GE is splitting three for two."

Buh-dump-bump. Is this a bubble or what?

Comment: An investor can switch from greed to fear in seconds. An active trader knows this.

9/11 did not change everything. If that were the case, you could say the Civil War changed everything, or say World War II changed everything, or say the atomic bomb changed everything.

Human psychology does not change. Meanings are in people, not events.

To some traders 9/11 was a time to sell. To some it was a buying opportunity. Captain Ron spent his time playing golf and now says, "Boats are merely a hole in the water where you throw money." And stubby is still stubby.

Trap 1

Insecurity Is the Enemy

Minimum Activity   0   1   2   3   4   5   6   7   8   Maximum Activity

A spy was caught in the Middle East. He was brought before the commandant, who said to him, "You know, of course, that the penalty for spying is death by firing squad." The spy asked the commandant whether he had any choices in the matter or whether there was anything he could say in his own behalf. The commandant replied, "Yes, you do have a choice. You can be shot by firing squad at dawn, or you can go through that door." He pointed to a large and ominous black door in the far corner of the room.

The spy asked what was behind the black door. The commandant answered, "That's for us to know. You decide: Is it the black door or the firing squad?" The spy requested time to come to a decision and was told that he had until dawn. One can imagine what he thought as he paced in his small cell throughout the night. It is likely that most of his thoughts were focused on the question, What could possibly be so horrible behind the black door that they would give me a choice?

In the morning he was brought before the commandant and asked for his decision. "Shoot me," he said. "At least I know what that is." After the spy was shot, a Red Cross observer who was present asked the commandant, "What was behind that black door?" The commandant replied, "Freedom."

The question on everyone's lips is, What is behind the other investment door? Why risk financial death when there is a plethora of investment options?

Trap 2

You Look Marvelous; You Look Too Marvelous

Minimum Activity 0 1 2 3 4 5 6 7 8 Maximum Activity

Charles Ponzi, an Italian immigrant, arrived in New York in 1893. He believed that the streets of America were paved with suckers eager to give up their hard-earned savings to anyone with a get-rich-quick scheme. He was right. Ponzi schemes capitalize on investor greed to attract new money to pay off early investors ... until the whole pyramid collapses. The word *Ponzi* has been used to describe our Social Security system as well as pension programs.

In June 1919, Charles Ponzi hit upon an idea that would make him rich. He called it the Ponzi Plan, but it was nothing more than the old Peter-to-Paul swindle. Ponzi undoubtedly had read about and researched this kind of swindle as it had been practiced by William Franklin Miller, who had operated the Miller Syndicate swindle in New York 20 years earlier.

Ponzi went to his friends and relatives and presented them with stacks of Postal Union coupons. "Each coupon," he told them, "can be purchased for the price of one penny. However, in Italy and other foreign countries they are redeemable for five cents each." He told them he was on his way to Italy to make the exchange. Each coupon would bring a 500 percent profit! They would all be millionaires within a few months. The concept was not logical, but the investors were gullible. To their amazement, within 90 days, little Charley reappeared, returning $750 interest on the investment. The investors were shocked. "Reinvest and tell your friends," Ponzi told his investors. They did, and within a few weeks the little Boston office Ponzi maintained was overrun with hundreds of eager, money-waving investors.

Ponzi knew how to dress. He even had a solid gold holder for his cigar. Today an Yves Saint Laurent silk jacket costs about $2,195; cotton velvet corded pants, $495; and an Armani white dress shirt, $450, and that includes the pocket square. Add a Prada tie, Calvin Klein socks, and Gucci shoes, and you are a walking investment. Oh, don't forget the Piaget watch. Remember the Ferengi rule of acquisition: "Don't trust anyone who dresses better than you." By the way, you will rarely see Giorgio Armani wearing an Armani suit.

If it looks too good to be true, it probably is.

Trap 3

Electronic Trading Has Trapdoors

By Mark Tinghino

Mark Tinghino has a BA in philosophy from the University of Illinois at Chicago and attended the University of Chicago as an MA/Ph.D. candidate in south Asian languages and civilization. He has published several magazine and online articles on trading and teaches trading seminars at the Chicago Board of Trade and the Chicago Mercantile Exchange. He has been a trader since 1983 and a commodity trading advisor (CTA) since 1987. In addition to being a CTA, he is an analyst with Worldwide Associates, LLC, in Chicago.

Minimum Activity									Maximum Activity
0	1	2	3	4	5	6	7	8	

Despite the "miracle" of nearly instantaneous fills and the elimination of the spreads between bid and ask prices, there are a number of caveats with respect to electronic markets. This material may not seem useful now, but as you progress from tyro to tycoon, it is a must read. If you don't understand it now, you will later.

Stop[1] Orders. On Globex,[2] stop limit orders are held on the Globex servers. As opposed to a stop order, which becomes

---

[1] An order that differs from a limit (price) order or market order in that the order is filled as soon as physically possible once the stop price is hit.

[2] Globex is the electronic futures market owned by the Chicago Mercantile Exchange.

a market order[3] when the stop price is hit, a market order is filled at any price as soon as there is a matching order to take the other side of the trade. A limit order can be filled only at your price or better. Therefore, if you use a limit order rather than a stop, that order may never get executed. Even worse is when equipment failure prevents your order from being transmitted over the Internet to Globex. In short, your order will be left twisting in the wind. Also, it is prudent to give your stop limit order some breathing room by placing the limit price at least a couple of ticks[4] away from the stop price. Otherwise, a fill in fast[5] markets may prove to be elusive or impossible.

Limit orders. Many times you will see your price traded without getting filled at your limit price. More likely than not, there are many orders queued up ahead of yours at the electronic exchange. Try setting your sights a tick or two lower or using market orders. That may not be a wise strategy for orders going to a pit,[6] but you do not run much of a risk of getting severely skidded[7] electronically. Placing only limit orders with unrealistic expectations could turn you into the equivalent of the poor sap who is constantly trying to reach

---

[3] A market order is filled as soon as physically possible regardless of the current price.

[4] A tick is the minimum price increment for a security or futures contract. For example, one tick on a minisized Dow contract at the Chicago Board of Trade's eCBOT electronic exchange is one point of the Dow Jones Industrial stock index valued at $5 per tick.

[5] A fast market is one in which price swings are both extreme and unusually rapid.

[6] A pit at a futures exchange is similar to a post at the New York Stock Exchange. Pits are typically octagon-shaped, with descending steps for access from the top level to the bottom level.

[7] Being skidded refers to the market moving through a price level by several ticks before a market or stop order eventually is filled.

the other side of the rainbow to acquire that ever-elusive pot of gold. If your limit order price is hit more than three times without a fill, it may be time to replace it with a market order or move it more within range of where the market currently is trading. Most well-designed trading platforms have such capabilities, and those are easy-to-use features with your keyboard or mouse.

Lot[8] *sizes and prices.* It is all too easy to assume that you entered your order correctly when using an electronic trading platform. If you accidentally list more shares, contracts, or options than you intend when entering a position or (perhaps even worse) fewer than you intend for a stop-loss order, you could sustain some unanticipated losses in your trading account. It would behoove one always to check every order very carefully before clicking one's mouse to send it off as well as every fill in one's positions or orders window for 100 percent accuracy.

The tendency to overtrade. The financial markets are not the arena for a trading video game. Treating them that way could make them the most expensive game you've ever played. If you want to try out some new or exotic trading strategy, you would be better off executing it in a simulated account unless you literally have money to burn.

---

[8] A standard lot in the stock market is 100 shares. Any smaller number of shares held is termed an odd lot. A lot in the futures or FOREX (cash currency foreign exchange market) is one contract.

Trap 4

Cramer vs. Kramer vs. Neal

Minimum Activity 0 1 2 3 4 5 6 7 8 Maximum Activity

When emotions take over, you react to rumors or buy what experts tell you to buy instead of doing your homework. Don't check your brains at the door when it comes to investing.

Look for the following:

1. A company that is number one or number two in a strong industry.
2. Earnings up 50 percent or more and accelerating for three quarters in a row.
3. Sales up at least 25 percent a quarter or accelerating. Without strong gains in sales, earnings won't hold up.
4. Return on equity (ROE) of 20 percent or more.
5. Profit margins that are among the highest in the industry.
6. Heavy trading volume at key buy points of a stock chart's price action, indicating that institutional investors are buying.
7. Leaders with relative price strength in the top 20 percent of the market.

Don't buy the "profits-don't-matter" baloney. Internet investors weren't the first to fall for it. Earnings matter and always will.

Follow when the market changes leadership. There are always industries heating up and industries cooling off. Look for the industries with highs. *Investor's Business Daily* reports that information every day.

Kramer was a character on *Seinfeld* who was always coming up with crazy investment schemes. The other Cramer is the *Mad Money* host on CNBC. These two K(C)ramers have one thing in common: They both have big money-making ideas, or is it money-making big ideas? However, there's a lesson to be learned from both: Always get a second opinion on any moneymaking scheme.

Trap 5

Skipping the Fundamentals Will Cost You

Minimum Activity   0   1   2   3   4   5   6   7   8   Maximum Activity

What Is Fundamental Analysis?

Fundamental analysis is based on the study of factors *external* to the trading markets that affect the supply and demand of a particular commodity in an attempt to predict future price movements. Such factors might include weather, the economy of a particular country, government policies, domestic and foreign political and economic events, and changing trade prospects.

Fundamental analysis theorizes that if one monitors relevant supply and demand factors for a particular commodity, a state of current or potential imbalance in the market may be identified that has not yet been reflected in the price level of that commodity. Fundamental analysis assumes that markets are imperfect, that information is not disseminated or assimilated instantaneously, and that econometric models can be constructed that generate equilibrium prices that may indicate that current prices are inconsistent with underlying economic conditions and thus will change in the future.

It is said that technicians will trade any market whereas fundamentalists will trade only a market they know. To a technician, a price or graph can be read the same way in just about any market.

69

To a fundamentalist, every market is different, with a myriad of supply and demand factors that must be sorted out to make a trading decision. It is no accident that many books and newsletters place a lot of emphasis on technical data and that one rarely sees articles on the fundamentals. This was not always the case. It is only recently that computers have replaced qualitative research done by analysts poring over supply and demand figures.

Taking It from the Top

The most popular and fruitful type of fundamental analysis is known as top-down analysis. This process first looks at the general economy, determining its characteristics and forecasting changes. Once this macro forecast is made, an analysis is done for the group of commodities that may rise or fall in the anticipated economic scenario.

At the final stage, the fundamentalist looks at the individual commodities and gives specific recommendations about the behavior of future prices. This method of analysis is called top-down because it deals with an analysis of a higher level of economic elements and then filters down to the specifics. By contrast, bottom-up analysis starts with the specific commodity and builds up to the commodity group and finally the economy in general. This is the type of analysis you usually hear from news reporters who must focus on a specific economic event and divine its whys and wherefores, often after a bad day in the market.

Price Pullbacks

The pullback of the last few years in the prices of consumer-driven commodities comes as no surprise to the fundamentalist. Consumers can react very rapidly to changes in income, employment, and interest rates. A family does not need to create a bar chart or Gann lines to determine whether increased purchases of red meat rather than chicken make economic sense. Eventually it will show up in the charts, but by that time it's usually common knowledge.

Although it is true that fundamentals are not the rage in the world of computers used by individual investors, there can be no doubt about their usefulness. Just pick up the business section of any newspaper. The papers are not filled with charts but with the who, what, where, when, and how of market movements. That is why fundamentals are important to the market.

Trap 6

Money for Nothing

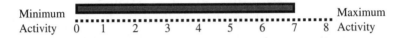

Minimum Activity 0 1 2 3 4 5 6 7 8 Maximum Activity

Before I left MTV to join the Disney Channel, we had a slogan: "I want my MTV." That slogan later found its way into the opening lyrics to a song by Dire Straits:

> Now look at them yo-yo's, that's the way you do it.
> You play the guitar on the MTV.
> That ain't workin', that's the way you do it. Money for nothin'
>   and chicks for free.
> Now that ain't workin', that's the way you do it. Lemme tell
>   ya them guys ain't dumb.
> Maybe get a blister on your little finger.
> Maybe get a blister on your thumb.

We've all seen the booklets with attention grabbers such as "How I turned $10,000 into $1 million in a year," "Get rich trading futures and options," and "Follow my XYZ system and you'll be on the path to financial independence." Welcome to the world of financial gurus, a circus boasting so many clowns and hucksters that even P.T. Barnum would be envious.

Oh, those videos did provide many of us with the basics for trading futures. One of my student traders, Michael, told me about one guru who caught his attention. His claim to fame was winning some trading championship back in the 1980s, before all the market whipsaws caused by today's technicians armed with megabytes of computing power.

Michael subscribed to his hotline, charted all his trades, and updated all his net profits and losses daily in an Excel spreadsheet to determine which markets he was hot in and which ones he wasn't. Months later, Michael took the plunge on one of his trade suggestions and did so in my trading account. Later, I realized I had gone long in a speculative demand market when industrial demand didn't support it. But now, it's Michael's turn to tell the rest of the story:

> Shortly afterward, I received more literature hawking the guru's "limited availability" $2,000 weekend seminar where he would "reveal his trading secrets." It showed six charts of his amazing trades; he magically entered and exited at the most profitable extremes. However, my Excel spreadsheets proved otherwise. I found he grossly exaggerated the results on five out of the six trades! From that point on, I was determined to get a solid education and steer clear of the charlatans.
>
> Living in Chicago definitely has its advantages. The Chicago Mercantile Exchange offers several futures courses, and after several months I had eight classes under my belt. I practically lived at the Merc library, reading anything from the simple $20 book to the exorbitantly priced $200 tell-alls— you know the ones. They're refilled with lots of big charts and oversized print. It took a while to separate the wheat from the chaff. But the real education started when I began meeting floor traders after the pits closed. Eventually, everything evolved into a trading plan.
>
> Nowadays, whenever I meet a novice enticed by some guru, I try to persuade him or her to take a few precautions before blindly following the guru's advice. Go to the Internet and search the guru's name in newsgroups, Usenet, or Deja News. Find out the real scoop from other traders' messages and save yourself some aggravation, time, and money. (I also do this with trading seminars, books, and brochures. I just love finding the truth behind those late-night infomercials.)

Ask the guru or his promotion company for an audited track record of his trades in the last few years. Contact the National Futures Association to dig up any dirt. Don't depend on your broker, as her commissions may depend on a guru's advisory service. Even if the guru checks out, track all his trades on a spreadsheet for three months while paper trading before committing any money.

Start cheap and avoid the scammers. If you do buy a guru's course, spend no more than $200, and do so only to learn the basics. After that, don't fall for the expensive add-on seminars. Most gurus feel the urge to write down their methods in an overpriced trading book anyway.

Beware of the jokers claiming to know how to make a fortune in a short time. They tend to rehash seasonals or recycle old overbought and oversold indicators such as stochastics and Relative Strength Index, RSI, or they create indicators based on common patterns and call them cute, funny names. You may learn a few tidbits, but you'll find that most of them are just system sellers, not actual traders.

Read books written by actual traders, not academics. There are several good ones out there, and I find my best signals come when several methodologies coincide. For a dose of reality, read Jack Schwagger's *Market Wizards* and *New Market Wizards*. Throughout both books, these real-life top traders all stress the importance of developing a good trading methodology and a trading plan that fits your personality, excellent money management skills requiring acceptable risk/reward ratios, and a disciplined approach to controlling losses and profits.

Prestidigitation 3

Full-Service Funds, or Should I Say Funs?

When I contacted Fidelity, I merely asked, "Are there any funds that increase in value as interest rates rise?" They replied, "Yes, they are listed under exchange traded funds."

Are there funds that increase as the stock market falls?

"Yes, the Rydex Fund."

Can I purchase a mutual fund for precious metals?

"Yes, we have that."

"Inflation scares me. Is there a way to hedge against that?"

"Yes, you can buy Treasury inflation-proof bonds or own them as a security."

As they say in the TD Waterhouse commercial, "You can do this."

Trap 7

$$y^2 = 2px$$

Minimum Activity 0 1 2 3 4 5 6 7 8 Maximum Activity

The formula is not a paradox; it is the formula for a parabola (see Figure P1-1). Many times, charts will go parabolic. If you are long, great. Look to take your profit, but hurry.

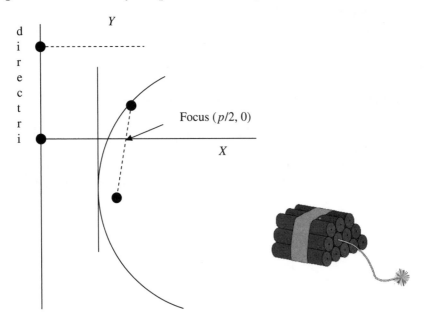

Figure P1-1 Formula for a Parabola

If you are not, you are in trouble, especially on the short or bear side.

Markets also can go parabolic on the down side.

Trap 8

Lisa Loves Russell

By Lisa Xu

Lisa Xu is the developer of the SSTT system that she uses in China and in the United States, the president of XY Financial Group, and an independent consultant in trading system development and portfolio management. To get a complete manual of Part 1: Basic SSTT System Applications and Part 2: Advanced SSTT System Applications, contact Lisa by e-mail at xyfinancial@msn.com.

Minimum Activity ▪▪▪▪▪▪▪▪▪▪▪▪▪▪▪▪▪▪▪▪▪▪▪ Maximum Activity

0 1 2 3 4 5 6 7 8

Among the minis, I love the Russell 2000. I love it to death because it moves big, nice, and smooth. It acts as a truthful bodyguard of Nasdaq; it follows Nasdaq right behind closely and never stops in the middle of the road and leaves you off the road. I just found out that this index has more than three times the trading volume and liquidity of the E-mini S&P.

I also have paid my dues for my mistakes in trading this index. Here are my mistakes and ways you can avoid them if you are one of the persons using my SSTT trading system:

Mistake 1. Do not run with a loss. Make it back right at where you fall.

Mistake 2. Do not be afraid of cutting the loss and reversing to win or break even.

Mistake 3. Do not leave your friend too early. Ride with your friend—the trend.

The market will be moving your way if you are *right* at the entering price. According to my basic system's rules, the right price means entering the long trade when the current buy signal price "B" is higher than the previous third buy signal price and going short if the current sell signal price (red down arrow) is below the previous third sell signal price.

Entering into the trade according to these rules results in three scenarios, as shown in the three charts that follow.

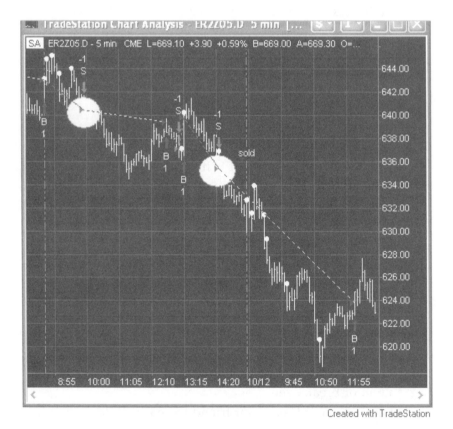

Created with TradeStation

Figure P1-2   Mini Russell 2000 Index Chart

MAKING A QUICK PROFIT   Figure P1-2 shows entering the market when the current sell signal is lower than the previous third sell signal price. The market continues to move down for a nice profit.

BREAKEVEN TRADE   In Figure P1-3, after entering a sell at 657.70, the market reversed to the upside. The buy signal comes out indicating a buy reversal, bought at 660.60, and a breakeven out at around 664.00.

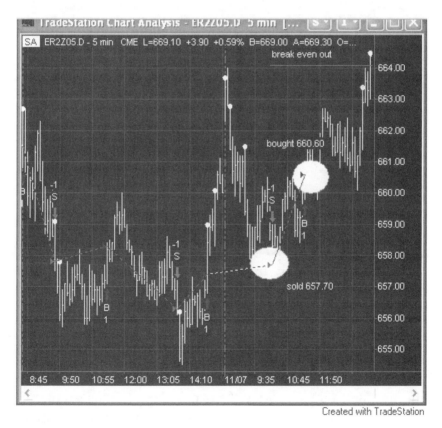

Created with TradeStation

Figure P1-3   Mini Russell 2000 Index Chart

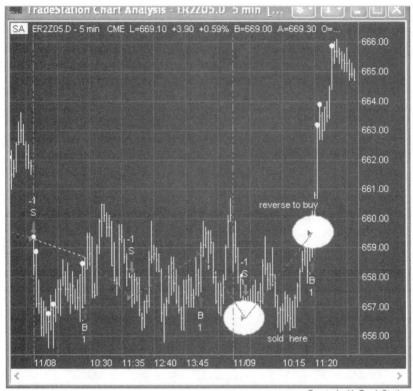

Created with TradeStation.

Figure P1-4   Mini Russell 2000 Index Chart

LOSE ONE AND MAKE TWO BACK TRADE   In Figure P1-4, after reversing to buy, the market moves dramatically to the upside, making the profit twice as much as the loss on the losing trade.

In these three situations, SSTT helps you pinpoint the entering price for profit and the price to cut the loss short and clearly signals the reversal price. The key in winning in the market is efficient, effective, and timely control of the risk. That sounds simple, and it is. My philosophy is to simplify everything in life, including trading; that way, the solution presents itself obviously.

Trap 9

The Stock Market Does Not Owe You a Living

Minimum · Maximur
Activity 0   1   2   3   4   5   6   7   8   Activity

Just because you invest, that does not mean the market owes you a living. The market is full of knaves who set traps for foolish investors.

You do not need to be 100 percent invested all the time.

If you are unsure, invest your money in bonds or cash. The highs of 1920 were not seen for nearly another 20 years. How long will it take to see the highs of the 1990s?

In *Life in the Crystal Palace*, Alan Harrington presented a penetrating view of large American corporations and coined the phrase "mobile truth." In a world of portable truth, you simply create a new view of the truth at each company.

Most company press releases are mobile truths.

It is as easy as switching channels. If you work for Coke, you claim it is the best drink in the world. If you switch jobs and go to work for Pepsi, you claim that that drink is totally awesome. Basically, the truth is a mercenary or soldier of fortune searching for the highest bidder.

Be a skeptic. You will never hear a mutual fund manager say, "If I were an owner of this fund, I would consider selling it."

Yeah, right! That'll be the day.

Trap 10

Message Boards

Minimum

Activity   0   1   2   3   4   5   6   7   8   Activity

Maximur Activity

It's easy to get carried away by message boards. Look at what one message board said about Home Depot and Hewlett-Packard in January 2000 and January 2006. What if you had acted on that advice? The logic seems correct. Do you care to guess where Home Depot is at this time? Care to guess where Home Depot is over six years later? The logic seems correct.

Home Depot Message Board January 2000

MESSAGE 1

Topic: Fresh Week   Good morning to all! No matter what Wall Street does to Home Depot stock, the company will keep on rocking. They are trying to say that it would be inflation-affected, but most here know that is just spin. HD makes it in both good and bad times. Roofs still go bad, toilets still break, water leaks still happen, and flooring still wears out.

People tend to repair what they own when the economy takes a downturn. Also, we have just gone through one of the largest new home purchase periods in history. New homes require a lot to get them where they are comfortable for the owner. They may slow down plans on improvement but will not stop those plans completely.

The decks still need to be waterproofed, the driveways need to be sealed, and the yard needs to be kept.

Home Depot (HD) is your all-season company, be it weather or the economy.

MESSAGE 2

If you go back and review HD charts of the last split, you will see that the stock went down for about 45 days and then shot up after the market had time to digest the split (it took about three months). I foresee that HD with its *market leadership crown* should do very well and think that it could split again later this year when the stock approaches the $90/share mark.

MESSAGE 3

HD stock may or may not run up; that remains to be seen. But over the past couple of years there have been a lot of stocks that were a better value than HD and haven't moved one bit. Unless the rules have changed, HD is looked upon by the market as a duopoly and is the number one company in that mix (with Lowe's being number two). They have only penetrated 20 percent of a $380 billion U.S. market and should increase their market share this coming year. Also, more important, HD's same store sales are rising 1 to 15 percent over previous years. I think HD has some more steam left and it is one of the best-managed firms in the U.S. Let's see how it goes.

MESSAGE 4

HD rating: Strong Buy, Target Price $105.00 by 6/25/00.

MESSAGE 5

I'm a novice HD investor but a "true believer" in HD stock.

Home Depot Message Board January 2006

MESSAGE 1

Enron movie will be out Tuesday.

MESSAGE 2

It is perhaps a good time now to open a six-pack and think about things for two hours while one learns how some things are done in a capitalist environment.

MESSAGE 3

A couple of bad managers will not bring this company down. What are these shysters?

MESSAGE 4

Nardelli, Donovan, and any other executives hired by Bob.

Langone.
Grasso.
The Board of Directors.

They are the ones stealing this company away from the stockholders.

MESSAGE 5

Throw my shoes down the stairs.

MESSAGE 6

Problem with vendor returns ... time to buy Lowe's.

MESSAGE 7

—That's what they said on CNBC. The big guy Leesman said, "This must be an anomaly."

But I received a postcard from home depot saying NO PAYMENTS NO INTEREST UNTIL 2007 IF YOU BUY THIS WEEK.

HMMM > ...

Hm ...

The so-called experts who you listen to for your investment advice were wrong again.

When you listen to pros and crooks with rosy projections and ignore cold hard facts, it can be hard on the wallet.

MESSAGE 8

Immediately, and I mean immediately, instruct the advertising department to pull all ads off all CNBC, NBC, and all their affiliate stations. If they want to use Home Depot as a whipping boy by showing some gang-banging thug crying about how he was wronged, then hit back and do it mercilessly. That CNBC would stoop this low to fill air time is repugnant. Sadly, it is to be expected from the type of sleaze ball "journalists" that exist today. Cramer, Faber, and Kernan are legends in their own minds. The only people that follow these television paparazzi are sick lazy demented fools in search of entertainment because they don't show Jerry Springer 24 hours a day.

The poor guy was made to inflate inventory numbers? Isn't that a shame? In one store? Well, the SEC should be very proud of itself on this one. I mean, their record in the last five years with Enron, Tyco, Adelphia, WorldCom, and countless others shows how focused they are on real fraud. Frigging unbelievable.

This pile stinks like manure!!!

—SEC starts informal Home Depot probe: report (HD) By Steve Goldstein LONDON (MarketWatch)—The Securities and Exchange

Commission has started an informal probe into whether The Home Depot Inc. (HD) collected inflated payments from suppliers to cover the cost of damaged merchandise, the *New York Post* reported Thursday. The payments, known as return-to-vendor charges, helped Home Depot pad store profit, according to current and former employees, the report said.

Trap 11

Don't Be Fooled by Randomness

Minimum  Maximum

Activity   0   1   2   3   4   5   6   7   8 Activity

Fooled by Randomness: The Hidden Role of Chance in the Markets and in Life is an underground sensation in the Chicago and New York markets. In Chicago we say, "If you're so rich, why are you so stupid?"

However, the important message by the author, Nassim Taleb, is that luck often is mistaken for being smart. The fact that you're in the right place at the right time may be a stroke of genius, but most likely it's dumb luck.

So what's a trader to do? If you make a windfall profit, "take the money and run." Also, if you buy a steel umbrella (and why would you?), don't use it during lightning storms out in an open field. The rules of randomness will not apply.

Prestidigitation 4

Trading the News

Minimum      Maximum
Activity   0   1   2   3   4   5   6   7   8   Activity

In addition to pivot points, traders trade fundamental news. Here is an approach used by active traders.

Assume that a key government report is scheduled and the analysts are anticipating a bullish report. Upon the release of the bullish report, if the market reacts in the opposite way, go in the direction of the market. This also can be used in a reverse situation: You simply go with the market. This may mean buying or selling with a market order.

Note that reports are not limited to official government releases but also can mean Treasury auctions that are anticipated during the day or even a highly touted press conference or comments by important officials whose actions may have a bearing on the market.

Also, keep in mind that the "news" contained in a report may already be reflected by current prices. This is the meaning of the market adage "Buy the rumor, sell the fact." In other words, you need to be alert about what is happening to supply and demand. Try to anticipate the effect on prices before it becomes "official" with an announcement. By the time a report confirms a fundamental factor, it usually is too late to become positioned. In fact, in many cases this may be a good time to take a position opposite to what the report would seem to indicate. Why? The market already has discounted what has become stale information. Once the news hits the news shows, it is too late.

Fundamentals may not be the darling of the industry, but they are important in outlining a trading strategy. Of course, fading a report is not infallible. The market still may have room to run in the direction suggested by the report, or technical signals may send a market beyond its actual value point because technicians "don't know any better."

You may choose to employ a technical approach to determine specific price entry and exit points. However, if you want to get on the same side of the trade as the "smart money," you must be able to see the big picture.

Part 2

Hardware, Operations, Software, and the Internet

If you think logging on means making a fire hotter, you should skip this section. If you hear the words *hard drive* and images of an eight-hour haul come to mind, skip this section. If a megahertz reminds you of back pain, you are not ready for computer trading.

Although a computer is an important tool for an active trader, your personal investment philosophy and strategies are more important. The investment in software will be substantial, and do you really think you know more than the professionals who trade for a living?

The top brokerage firms have research departments that are second to none. You can use your computer simply to compare and contrast trading ideas. Do really need up-to-the-second real-time prices? Does your broker supply many of the tools you need at no charge? Is it really worth the investment? Will it give you an edge?

This section describes the optimum conditions you need to be an active trader. Once you enter the high-tech world of "active trading," you are in a realm inhabitated by viruses, hacks, crashes, bugs, and power failures. Any trade you make is your responsibility. There is no broker to save you.

Decide how much computer power you really need. There's nothing wrong with flying a piper cub before you become Rocket Man.

I wish to thank Michael Harris for his assistance with this section.

Michael is the President of International Services Incorporated based in Evanston, Illinois. International Services develops Internet-based business solutions for the international banking and media industries. Born in 1952, Michael earned his bachelor's degree in engineering from Ohio State University in 1980. He participated in coursework towards a master's degree in artificial intelligence. He has worked in the information technology industry for over 25 years as a programmer, systems analyst, and business systems developer. In a recent position as CTO, he wrote a patent for an information management system for compressing and managing data at the binary level. Michael can be reached by e-mail: isiglobal@gmail.com.

Hardware

Tip 1

The Real Commitment

Minimum Activity   0   1   2   3   4   5   6   7   8   Maximum Activity

The computer hardware used for active trading is unique and has to be configured specially to meet the requirements for speed, performance, and reliability in trading. Active traders should expect to spend at least $5,000 to assemble the computer hardware and software needed to create a reliable trading platform. However, you should start smaller. You can always add software.

The next area of commitment is time. An active trader should spend enough time to learn how to use his or her computer hardware and software as well as conduct market research on the Web, develop trading strategies, and continuously monitor the markets for trading opportunities. The mastery of a personal trading technique can take months to perfect; therefore, it is necessary to commit enough time to be successful.

Use of Computers for Active Trading

Twas brillig, and the slithy toves
Did gyre and gimble in the wabe:
All mimsy were the borogoves,
And the mome raths outgrabe.

From *Through the Looking-Glass and What Alice Found There*, 1872, by Lewis Carroll

Computers are complex, and if you don't speak the computer Jabberwocky, you will be lost as an active trader! The use of computers in active trading is absolutely crucial, and mastery of their use is imperative. There has been a progression from the "open outcry" floor trading system used in the past by exchanges to a heavy reliance on computers today. Trading arcades and individual active traders now use computers to buy and sell stocks, options, and futures. Further, automated computer programs are being used by trading arcades and institutional investors to make trades under human supervision.

Because there is so much at risk in active trading, an active trader must achieve a high level of proficiency in the use of computer hardware and software, telecommunications, and the Web. Forget about getting customer support to help you in the middle of a trade. To achieve the required level of proficiency, an active trader should embark on a serious path of education. Recommended educational sources include institutions that offer certified computer courses and grant a certificate of course credit. This level of education will help you achieve a quality standard that allows you to operate a computer. Computer-based courses are offered by community colleges and universities specializing in teaching the basics of computer hardware and software and telecommunications.

It is also a good idea to find a "computer guru" to assist you in the higher-level use of a computer. This does not mean relying on your 16-year-old nephew who has played computer games since he was 5 years old. It means finding someone with the demonstrated maturity and familiarity with computers to understand how computer hardware and software and telecommunications interact. This person is your ally and sounding board, perhaps a fellow active trader. It is impossible for any individual to master all aspects of computer operation because the technology is complex and constantly changing. The best you can hope to do is to stay current on the use of your computer as a trading platform and find a computer guru to consult when necessary.

Warning

If you do not have the time to learn how to use a computer and the associated application software for active trading, use a familiar low-technology device: the telephone. In other words, call your broker to make your trades. It is your time and money. Spend it wisely.

There is no relationship between how often you trade and being financially successful. As you move up the continuum to being more active, you are taking more risk. Be sure you have a trading edge that requires a computer and software. Very few people beat the market on a consistent basis. Those who do reach "rock star" status.

Disclaimer

Because of the many combinations of hardware and software, it is necessary to warn the reader that we do not guarantee results from using this information. Computer hardware and software are subject to changes in specifications and configurations. These are general guidelines of operation and are derived from commonly available knowledge.

Tip 2

PC Pioneers Can Be Led Astray

Minimum Activity   0   1   2   3   4   5   6   7   8   Maximum Activity

Finding the optimal computer for active trading is a challenge. The first impulse is to purchase the fastest and highest-performance computer system possible for the lowest price. Why not? Surely the rules of purchase optimization apply. Not always!

Computer hardware, especially the central processing unit (CPU), usually leads software development. The CPU is the central "brain" of the computer that controls all the computer's functions. Typically, Microsoft releases operating system (OS) versions two years behind Intel's semiconductor technology. Buying a new computer featuring a "32-bit CPU" initially may appear to be a good idea. However, if the OS or the trading software application can process only in 16-bit units, the advantage of having a 32-bit CPU is wasted until it matches the software's processing capacity.

The main reason for the software industry lag is that the CPU manufacturing market has a shorter product life cycle and takes advantage of the mass production techniques used to make a standard chip. The CPU design is tested and finalized, and then factories produce millions for installation into computers.

In contrast, the software development life cycle is much longer because of the extensive testing necessary for the interaction of numerous software applications. Although the "alpha" internal testing of software may be complete, the "beta" version of the software must be tested in the actual marketplace. When the marketplace finds problems, the software developer must make the necessary changes and issue an updated version of the software. This is one reason Microsoft continuously updates the OS online.

An active trader should upgrade PC hardware only if it matches the software in use. This will let you avoid pioneering a wrong and expensive path.

Note: The number of bits processed by the computer CPU, known as a *word*, should not to be confused with the CPU's speed. See Trick 3: The Need for CPU Speed.

Tip 3

To PC or Mac, That Is the Question

Minimum Activity									Maximum Activity
	0	1	2	3	4	5	6	7	8

Macs are excellent graphics computers; however, there are major challenges in using a Mac for active trading. First, Macs use a CPU that is designed to run only Mac software. In comparison to a PC, the software available for a Mac is minimal, and the software for active trading is even less developed. Admittedly, it is possible to run PC software in emulation mode on a Mac, but the computing performance is compromised in terms of speed, and therefore it is not suitable for implementing rapid trades.

Second, the majority of software written for active trading runs on a PC-based platform. The major reason for this is that 99.99 percent of the world uses PCs for a wide variety of applications. Consequently, software developers write applications for the largest market: the PC. Further, the support available for PC-based software applications is proportionally larger than that for the Mac, especially for an active trader.

In June 2005, Apple announced that it would be switching its CPU chip to an Intel-based architecture. What does this mean to active traders? Not much. For anyone considering using a Mac for trading, it could be a disaster to wait for the new Macs to be ready or to be compatible with a PC. In addition, the alpha and beta testing of new active trading software for the Intel-based CPU Mac chip may extend into the unknown future.

Tip 4

Laptops Will Actually Grow Legs and Walk

Minimum Activity   0   1   2   3   4   5   6   7   8   Maximum Activity

If an active trader spent a portion of his or her time and money protecting a laptop computer from theft, the return on that investment would be well worth it. Laptops should not be taken out in public unless it is absolutely necessary to do so. Statistics show that an unattended laptop is very attractive to a thief. The cost of a laptop is higher than that of a desktop, and even though you may have the laptop insured, it is the information on the computer that makes it valuable. In the wrong hands, your information could lead to identity theft and, in the case of an active trader, exposure to even greater losses if the thief used your trading account.

PC Theft and Recovery Statistics

- Total laptop theft losses for 2004 increased to more than $6.7 million—CSI/FBI Computer Crime and Security Survey, 2004
- More than 600,000 PCs were stolen in 2003, and theft ranks as the number two cause for overall PC loss—Safeware Insurance Agency 2003
- Laptop theft was associated with 59 percent of computer attacks in government agencies, corporations, and universities during 2003—Baseline 2004

- Computer crime statistics reveal that approximately 80 percent of computer crime consists of "inside jobs" by disgrun-
  tled employees and that 73 percent of companies do not have
  specific security policies for their laptop computers—Gartner
  Group 2003
- Ninety-seven percent of stolen computers are never recov-
  ered. The average company's loss from laptop theft is more
  than $47,000—CSI/FBI Computer Crime and Security
  Survey, 2003

Some active traders may believe that trading with a laptop at a
fashionable "wireless hotspot" is a status symbol. However, if the
laptop is knocked onto the floor, a liquid is spilled on it, or it is
stolen, the fashion will soon fade. If you are serious about using a
laptop for active trading, be careful how and where you use it.

Note: To stay current on this topic, search the Web using the
search term "laptop theft statistics."

Tip 5

Monitoring Your Trading World

Minimum Activity   0   1   2   3   4   5   6   7   8   Maximum Activity

To set up an active trading system that would command the respect of NASA Mission Control, you should have at least two monitors to display diverse trading information. Some active traders use up to nine monitors to show extremely diverse real-time market information; the number of monitors necessary is determined by your need for information. Be sure that your trading computer can support the number of required monitors.

There are two types of monitors available: VGA (analog) and DVI (digital). All monitors support VGA, and only a few LCD monitors support DVI. Often, DVI provides better resolution than VGA. Choose a monitor at least 19 inches in diagonal measurement and view the display before you buy it.

Flat panel monitors smaller than 19 inches do not have the resolution needed by an active trader. LCD monitors should have at least a 1280 × 1024 pixel display area. Pixels are the small dots on a monitor screen that display the image you see. Larger monitors provide more pixels; however, they do not necessarily provide higher resolution per viewing area.

Be aware that the some monitors use the old television technology with a cathode ray tube (CRT) to generate the display image on the screen. CRT monitors produce more electromagnetic radiation than LCD monitors and tend to have a less crisp screen image. In comparison, LCD monitors are a superior choice for active traders because the higher resolution in the display causes less visual fatigue over time.

Note: To stay current on this topic, search the Web using the search term "high-resolution monitor."

Trick 1

Be a Flasher

Minimum Activity 0 1 2 3 4 5 6 7 8 Maximum Activity

A flash memory drive is a small solid-state memory drive that is comparable to a hard drive; it connects to a computer directly through a Universal Serial Bus (USB) port on a PC. It is remarkably small, about the size of a felt-tip marker. Its main advantage is its size and ability to store large amounts of information. Secondarily, it does not have any moving parts to break down, as in a typical hard drive. It is used primarily to transfer files between PCs. Flash drives can hold any type of data, such as Excel, jpeg, video, and text files. Flash drives also are referred to as key drives, thumb drives, jump drives, USB drives, memory sticks, and pen drives.

Flash drives are compact and easy-to-use devices that are smaller than portable disks and can be acquired in memory sizes up to 16 gigabytes. They slip easily into your pocket or can be worn conveniently around your neck or on a key chain for the ultimate in portable storage. Flash drives fulfill the real promise of the digital age: complete freedom and mobility of data. The differences between flash drives are mostly in price, capacity, design, functions, and features. What is really important is that they're all pluggable, portable, and powerful.

How can active traders use a flash drive? Use your imagination. Try the following tricks:

- Now you transport your information, not your laptop computer. Simply transfer the information of interest to the flash drive, take it to a computer at another location, and plug it into the USB port of the other computer. Now you are ready to transfer and access your information immediately.

- Flash drives hold gigabytes of data. This means you can store hundreds of thousands of trading research reports, Excel spreadsheets, Word documents, and so on. This permits you to consolidate your information and transport it.
- If you share a computer, flash drives are a great way to store trade-related information. Use the flash drive instead of using the computer's hard drive to store your information. When you are done with the computer, remove the flash drive with your information and leave no trace of the information that was processed by the computer.
- According to some manufacturers' specifications, flash drives can maintain data for 10 years. In that period, you probably will have to replace your computer hard drive two times. Now an active trader can back up crucial trade information on the flash drive and never worry about when the hard disk will fail.
- Create a word-processed file stating who owns the flash drive and save it on the flash drive itself. If you lose the flash drive, there is a way for the finder to contact you.

Trick 2

Improve Your Screen Image

During an active trader's online session, it is often necessary to capture information displayed on the screen. Various active trader software applications from brokers such as Fidelity, Ameritrade, and Charles Schwab offer the ability to store data associated with a trade. Trade data may consist of real-time streaming quotes, chart data, account balances, and the like. Typically, an active trader can retrieve this information in the form of a data file for printing out or exporting to a spreadsheet. However, these applications often do not provide the ability to capture the actual screen image being displayed on the computer monitor at a crucial moment.

A simple trick can be used by an active trader to capture the image being displayed on the monitor. When the monitor displays a screen of interest to you, simultaneously push the "CTRL" and "Print Screen/SysRq" keys. CTRL usually is found in the lower right and left sections of the keyboard. Screen/SysRq usually is situated in the upper-right-hand section of the keyboard. When you push these keys simultaneously, the image displayed on the screen at that moment is captured automatically in the computer memory buffer, making it available for pasting into another software application.

The next step in this trick is to open the software application to which you wish to paste the captured image, such as Word. Click on the standard "Edit" menu choice and display the drop-down menu. Click on the "Paste" label, and the image is pasted into the document. This trick permits you to keep a constant graphic image record of any real-time screen event. These images can be captured and pasted into a word-processing document consecutively and serve as a continuous historical record of the trade.

This is a "one-time" process, and so only one image can be captured and pasted at a time. When you capture another image by simultaneously pressing the CTRL and Print Screen/SysRq keys again, the previous image is lost and replaced by the current captured image. Further, the image cannot be edited with a word processor; however, it can be edited with a graphic software application such as PhotoShop, MS-Paint, or MS-FrontPage. Now an active trader can capture the history of a trade in screen images and refer to them later for research purposes.

Trick 3

The Need for CPU Speed

Minimum Activity									Maximum Activity
	0	1	2	3	4	5	6	7	8

A major concern of active traders is the speed of executing a trade. One factor in the trade execution speed equation is the speed of the CPU. The other factor in the equation is the speed of the telecommunication link to the broker. (See Tip 3: The Need for Connection Speed in the section on the Internet.) CPU speed is measured in pulses per second, known as Hertz (Hz) units. If the speed of a CPU is 1 gigahertz, meaning 1 billion pulses per second, a 2-gigahertz CPU will process information twice as fast. An analogy is traveling on a highway: If you drive twice as fast, you will get there in half the time. This translates to a software application running twice as fast on a 2-gigahertz CPU. For active traders, faster is better, especially in using software applications for statistical analysis, plotting market trends, doing historical analysis, and so on. The faster you are able to derive crucial information to make an intelligent trade, the better.

All computers are not created equal. There are computers built especially for active traders, and it is recommended that you research this market to find the best trading computer for your overall needs. Several considerations should be made in choosing CPU speed. First, get the CPU with the fastest speed. Second, get a computer with dual processors. The advantage of using dual processors is that it will permit you to split data processing between two CPUs and in some cases permit you to process data at an even more accelerated rate. This is possible because the computing is shared between two processors. Another advantage of a dual processor is that if one processor fails, the other will perform the computing task until the computer can be repaired. This is valuable feature when you are in the middle of a trade.

Trap 1

If You Don't Know, Don't Fix It

Minimum
Activity   0   1   2   3   4   5   6   7   8   Maximum Activity

A computer used exclusively for active trading utilizes hardware and software configurations above those used in a normal PC. Don't get caught not knowing the basics. Be sure to get a computer that is capable of performing a wide variety of tasks quickly and is reliable. An active trader should be aware of the basic components when assembling computer hardware and software for active trading, and the computer should have the following minimal system specifications:

- *CPU processor*. Stay with standard CPU configurations such as an Intel Pentium 4 or higher when they are available. The CPU should include the Intel chipset with at least a 32-bit processor. Be aware of when new CPU processors become available and make sure they are compatible with your trading application software.
- *CPU speed*. Use at least a 3.0-GHz CPU or get a faster one if possible. A faster CPU is useful for traders who are interested in back testing their ideas. Charts and graphs will calculate and open faster.
- *Random-access memory*. Use at least a 1-gigabyte random-access memory (RAM) cache. The memory cache is where your software application is loaded to run its task. The more software applications you run simultaneously, the more RAM will be needed. You may use more memory if you plan

109

for additional specialized software, but be aware that when you order more than 2 GB of memory, not all of the memory will be usable because of motherboard resource limitations, a common problem with all single-CPU motherboards and some dual-processor CPUs.

- *Hard drive*. At least 100 gigabytes.
- *Floppy drive*. Used primarily for copying small files or an emergency boot.
- *CD read and write drive*. Used for loading software and making CD backups.
- *Video display monitor support*. It is common for an active trader to display a variety of diverse information sources related to a trade. The trading computer should support at least four video display monitors simultaneously. In some cases you may wish to have up to six monitors. Be sure that the computer can drive these display monitors without compromising the speed of the CPU.
- *Operating system*. Windows XP Professional is able to support the majority of active trading software. Install all new OS updates as they become available.
- *Power supply*. Use a heavy-duty power supply. The power supply provides electrical power to the computer and commonly fails over the years of use. A heavy-duty power supply will have longer life, but it should be replaced in the course of preventive maintenance after three years of use.
- *Heat dissipation*. Make sure the CPU has "heat spreaders" to dissipate the heat generated by the CPU and other hardware components. Heat is a destroyer of computers, and if it is not dissipated, it will lead to rapid computer failure. This also is recommended for traders working in rooms that lack air-conditioning or placing significant sustained demands on the CPU.

NOTES

1. One reliable source for computers built especially for active traders is www.tradingcomputers.com. Call toll-free at 800-435-1094.
2. To stay current on this topic, search the Web using the search term "trading computer."

Trap 2

Be Careful When You Back Up

Minimum Activity   0   1   2   3   4   5   6   7   8   Maximum Activity

Two heads are better than one. However, are three heads better than two? Absolutely!

If you are an active trader, segmenting the use of your computers is mandatory. Computers can be used for a wide variety of applications; however, for an active trader, the application is clear: to make the trade! Therefore, by segmenting the computers into specific functions, you can maintain the quality of each computing environment.

There are three basic types of computing environments.

Your Trading Computer

This is your baby. No one should use it except you, and only for trading. It should be password-protected and under your total control. It represents the optimal environment for active trading and is built for speed and ability to make the trade. It should be used to run only software applications related to active trading. High-speed connections should be used for trading only. A Web browser such as Internet Explorer or Firefox should be used only in the course of a trade in order to avoid viruses. It should not have an e-mail client such as Microsoft Outlook or Eudora, because this is a vector for viruses to infect your computing environment, resulting in potential damage to your software or computer.

Your Backup and Operations Computer

This is your second baby. It should have the same hardware and software configuration as your trading computer. It functions to back up the trading computer, conduct research, and communicate. After you back up your trading computer data files to a storage medium such as a CD or a USB flash drive, you can transfer those files to your backup and operations computer. This is important because if your trading computer fails, you can use the backup and operations computer to make trades until the trading computer is repaired.

All market research done on the Web should be conducted and stored on this computer. Additional research, such as running statistical analysis software or spreadsheets, also can be done on this computer without taking up the valuable computing resources of your trading computer.

Communication via e-mail, Webmail, instant messaging, and the like, can be conducted safely with your broker or fellow traders without taking the chance of infecting your trading computer.

It is possible to share monitor displays between the trading computer and the backup and operations computer if all the monitors are not in demand by the trading computer.

Your Home Computer

This is the shared baby. All software not related to active trading can be placed on this computer without fear of jeopardizing your trading computer environment. To avoid the most challenging difficulties, such as America Online (AOL) pop-up advertisements appearing in the middle of a trade, keep your three heads separated.

Trap 3

The Abyss

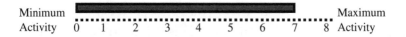

Minimum Activity 0 1 2 3 4 5 6 7 8 Maximum Activity

Wi-Fi is an abbreviation for the words *wireless fidelity*. It is known technically as the 802.11 network. The main value of Wi-Fi is that it allows you to connect your desktop or laptop computer to the Internet without using wires. The Wi-Fi network consists primarily of a base station connected to the Internet. The base station transmits the Internet signal to a receiver in your computer. The average range of the base station transmitter is approximately 1,000 feet and is influenced by transmitter power, antenna length, and the density of obstructions between the transmitter and the receiver, such as building walls. The growth in Wi-Fi popularity has been augmented by the freedom of mobile computing allowed by being wireless. This popularity has extended into the home, the office, and even the public sector, permitting Wi-Fi access in libraries, coffee shops, and everywhere in several major cities.

However, to an active trader, what appears to be the ultimate answer in mobile trading has a hidden problem: security. The use of wireless access to the Internet simultaneously creates the problem that anyone can access it unless certain security precautions are taken. Typically, when a Wi-Fi network is installed in the home, office, or public sector, very few of the security features are activated.

Wi-Fi networks are susceptible to being compromised because the Wi-Fi signal can be accessed by hackers, criminals, or even freeloaders using your Wi-Fi network for Internet access. After hackers gain access to your Wi-Fi network, they not only can slow down your Internet connection but can monitor your computer and in the worst case steal information without your knowing it. Current studies indicate that the majority of home Wi-Fi networks do not have sufficient protection from outside hackers. According to the research firm Gartner, 80 percent of residential Wi-Fi networks are unsecured, and 70 percent of successful attacks on wireless systems in 2006 were the result of mismanaged networks. The major threat to a Wi-Fi network is a hacker attack to implant malware programs, such as spyware, adware, and viruses.

Here is a list of the major Wi-Fi features that need to be activated when one is installing and using a Wi-Fi network at home, in the office, or in the public sector:

1. *Password protection.* Most Wi-Fi networks have passwords that the user must enter before access to the network is granted. The manufacturer uses a standard password such as "admin," but during installation this needs to be changed. Changing the default password will prevent hackers from accessing the Wi-Fi network.

2. *Machine Address Code.* The Wi-Fi network can control which computers are able to access the network. Every computer has a unique Machine Address Code (MAC) built in to identify it. This code can be registered on the Wi-Fi network as having access. This is one of the strongest methods to control a Wi-Fi network.

3. *Encryption.* Wi-Fi networks have an encryption function called Wired Equivalent Privacy (WEP) that converts a meaningful transmission over the network into scrambled nonsense. Setting up the WEP is technical and may require a technician to implement the solution correctly. However,

once it has been set up, you can be assured of exclusive access without broadcasting your every keystroke to the world.

4. *Disabling SSID*. Wi-Fi networks are configured to broadcast a Service Set Identifier (SSID). The SSID is broadcast every few seconds to indicate that the Wi-Fi network is available for Internet access. The SSID is broadcast as the name of your Wi-Fi network, such as "MyWiFi." This name will appear on any computer set up to receive a Wi-Fi signal. However, after your network is set up, disable SSID to avoid access by unauthorized users.

Public Wi-Fi Access

Home and office Wi-Fi networks can be secured, but what about public Wi-Fi networks available in a hotel, airport, café, or any other hotspot? Most hotspots do not activate security features such as passwords, encryption, and WEP because it would make it difficult to access the network.

A Warning to Wi-Fi Laptop Users

A popular hotspot could conceal hackers, criminals, and identity thieves just waiting for you to access the network with your laptop. A recent report issued by the security vendor Fortinet Inc. stated that "most mobile users do not realize that once connected to a wireless hotspot, they become a member of a connected community of users—most or all of whom are strangers. This poses significant security risks as there is often little or no control of what can pass from user to user via a wireless access point, and that can have disastrous consequences."

Disastrous consequences while drinking a café au lait? Yes, a laptop user easily can pick up malware, such as a virus or a worm, while connected to a Wi-Fi network. The malware then could be transferred to the home or office Wi-Fi network when the user returns there. To avoid this public exposure, be sure to have firewall and an antimalware software installed on your computer to detect and stop malware.

The latest Wi-Fi features, when activated, reduce the chance of infection by malware over the Wi-Fi network, and new enhancements to Wi-Fi security in 2006 were designed to make it easier for users to install and use to protect their computers from attack.

Operations

Tip 1

People First, Computer Second

Minimum  Maximum
Activity 0   1   2   3   4   5   6   7   8 Activity

The date was September 10, 2001. The computers and software used to analyze trading conditions and execute trades were operating normally. Institutional traders, arcade traders, and active traders were trading normally. It seemed like just another trading day. On September 11, 2001, tragedy struck. The United States was under a surprise terrorist attack. Wall Street shut down after two planes crashed into the World Trade Center. Downtown New York City, including the financial center, was a war zone. All trading was suspended at the New York Stock Exchange. The Nasdaq market was considering whether to open. The American Stock Exchange, New York Mercantile Exchange, and World Trade Center were evacuated. A similar attack on the Pentagon was underway.

The computers and software used to analyze trading conditions and execute trades were operating normally. However, institutional traders, arcade traders, and active traders were in a panic. Why the discrepancy?

The markets are based on people first and computers second. All the analytical computer systems and trading systems in use could not predict the 9/11 events. It was the people operating those systems who suspended trading, not the computer software.

Another example of how strongly people influence trading is the way they perceive the weather. When the Weather Channel broadcasts the emergence of a tropical storm off the coast of Florida, it is the perception by people of this event that will influence the markets. The storm could develop into a hurricane and devastate the orange tree orchards, affecting the harvesting of oranges and ultimately the availability of orange juice. Therefore, it is people who analyze the weather and interpret it as a call on the price of oranges going up in the marketplace.

People influence the markets, and traders develop a feel for the market that a computer system cannot match. Psychological perceptions also can influence the market independently of statistical analysis of the market data. If you can understand how the market is going to move, you have developed your own personal system. Trade when you have your strategic edge and reduce the risk. You will know when an elephant enters the room; however, the computer will act as if nothing had happened.

There are hundreds of strategies to trade, and each of those strategies involves people and their perceptions. Admittedly, mathematical and computer-based analysis can be used to arrive at logical conclusions to assist an active trader in making a decision. However, it is the human element that understands the advantage in active trading.

Tip 2

Get Out of the Slow Lane

Minimum Activity      Maximum Activity

0   1   2   3   4   5   6   7   8

An active trader needs optimal computer performance to maintain his or her edge in trading. However, every time you use your computer, it will get progressively slower. Why? There are many causes of slow performance, and it is necessary to maintain your computer constantly as you would do with any other machine built for speed. The major causes of degradation in computer performance are listed below, and a maintenance plan should be implemented to maintain your computer's performance.

Defragment the Hard Drive

All the information created by you is stored continuously on the hard drive. Each time you save a file to the hard disk, it writes the data in a progressive sequence. However, as you use different software applications, the data are saved in different locations on the drive. When you access the data, the computer must search the entire hard drive to find where the data were stored. This process takes longer as the hard drive space is used. To avoid this problem, it is necessary periodically to defragment the hard drive by using the Microsoft Windows Defragment Program. You can find it by clicking on "Start—Programs—Accessories—Systems Tools—Disk Defragmenter."

Use Antispyware

Spyware is a software application that is downloaded unintentionally through spam e-mail or Web sites featuring "free" screen savers or animated icons for your computer desktop. The sole purpose of spyware is to monitor and report what you are doing on your computer to a data-gathering facility. Data on your computer, such as your word-processed documents, are sent periodically to the originator of the spyware. Spyware can slow the performance of your computer, and all precautions should be taken to avoid being infected.

The following free antispyware programs are recommended to provide protection from various types of spyware:

AdAware. Download from www.lavasoftusa.com.
SpyBot Search & Destroy. Download from
   www.safer-networking.org.
Microsoft Anti-Spyware. Download from
   www.microsoft.com/spyware.

Although you should defragment monthly, these three antispyware software applications should be run in sequence at least weekly or as often as you believe it is necessary. Maintaining your computer at an optimal performance level not only will help your speed in trading, it also will help you avoid progressive degradation in computer performance.

Tip 3

Avoid Spam or End Up Eating It

Minimum Activity  Maximum Activity

0   1   2   3   4   5   6   7   8

The word *spam* used to be associated with a ham product savored by some and scorned by others. The word *spam* as defined by computer users means any unsolicited e-mail. In comparison to the volume of regular surface mail, the presence of unsolicited mail was bearable. However, in the Internet world, spam is a serious and growing threat to e-mail communication.

Why? Spam is not only a waste of Internet bandwidth, computer hard disk storage, and even computer processing power. It is also a waste of an active trader's most valuable asset: *time*.

A Few Spam E-Mail Statistics

According to www.appriver.com, 75 percent of global Internet traffic is spam, with a growth rate of 20 percent per year. Most of the spam is concentrated around holidays, and as you can imagine, with this enormous growth rate, the majority of Internet traffic will be spam at some point.

America Online estimates that spam already accounts for more than 30 percent of the e-mail sent to its members: as many as 24 million messages a day. There are 250,000 spam-related complaints reported every day at AOL alone.

PC MAGAZINE   According to *PC*, 74 percent of customers believe that their ISPs should be responsible for fixing spam problems, and 7 percent of ISP processing is directly attributable to spam.

GARTNER GROUP   According to the Gartner Group, nearly $2 of each customer's monthly bill can be attributed to the cost of connect time used to download spam.

INFORMATION WEEK   How can the active trader avoid this growing problem? According to *Information Week*, not easily. However, there are certain steps you can take to reduce the amount of spam you receive:

1. Create a personal e-mail account for private use only. Limit the distribution of this address
2. Create a Web-based e-mail account with an e-mail provider such as Yahoo, Google, or Hotmail to serve as your public e-mail box. Direct general e-mail correspondence to this Web-based account.
3. Use additional spam-blocking software such as Mailwasher, Spamkiller, and Ella to block spam.
4. Use an Internet Service Provider that has a strong spam filter. Use an e-mail client such as Outlook or Eudora to set up spam filters to block spam missed by the ISP.

Note: To stay current on this topic, search the Web using the search term "stop spam."

Tip 4

It's Not Your Father's E-Mail Anymore

Minimum Activity 0 1 2 3 4 5 6 7 8 Maximum Activity

E-mail has become the lifeblood of modern communication. If you are an active trader, e-mail will be your primary form of written communication with your broker, business associates, technical support, and so forth. You must master this form of communication to interact with the trading community.

E-Mail Usage Statistics

"It has been estimated that the average business e-mail user sends and receives about 19,000 e-mails each year and that the average e-mail database will grow by 37 percent each year."—Osterman Research 2004

The technology research firm IDC estimates that by 2005, "U.S. businesses will send a staggering 35 billion e-mails each day. Indeed, a survey of corporate executives by the research firm META Group Inc. found that electronic mail is now more important to business operations than phone service."

E-mail is here to stay, and you must master the basics of its use to function as an active trader. The following e-mail basics are guidelines for its use.

E-Mail Headers

To. Used for the primary recipient's e-mail address. Multiple
e-mail addresses can be added and separated by semicolons.

cc. Used for sending a courtesy copy to additional recipients.
Multiple e-mail addresses can be added and separated by
semicolons.

bcc. Used for sending a "blind courtesy copy" to additional
recipients, without the "to" and "cc" recipients knowing to
whom you are sending a copy of the e-mail. Multiple e-mail
addresses can be added and separated by semicolons.

Note: It is often a good policy to use the "bcc" header to contain
your own e-mail address. This will serve to supply a copy for your
own records of the e-mails that you sent.

Dangerous E-Mail

One of the most dangerous aspects of e-mail is not technological
but human. From the beginning of time, people have relied on the
written word as a form of reliable communication. However,
because there is not a definitive solution in place to assure the
veracity of e-mail and because malware can be attached to an
e-mail message, the credibility of e-mail can be compromised
severely.

Be aware of the following types of dangerous e-mail:

SCAM   This is an age-old trick in a new medium. For example,
the e-mail will be sent from an unknown source such as a company,
bank, or marketing group, asking you for personal information
such as your bank account number, Social Security number, or
password.

PHISHING   The e-mail will appear to come from a legitimate organization such as a bank, maybe even your bank. In reality, it is an attempt to gather your personal account information under a false identity.

SPOOFING   You might receive e-mail from someone you know or, in the most ridiculous situation, e-mail from yourself. How does this happen? The spoofer obtains a real e-mail address from hacking activity or by monitoring Internet traffic. A special modification to an e-mail program makes it possible to create a false identity for the sender. When you receive this type of e-mail, it initially appears credible. However, after you read the e-mail, it becomes obvious that the sender is a spoof of a real e-mail address.

E-MAIL ATTACHMENTS   E-mail attachments are files that are attached to an e-mail message. E-mail attachments can be dangerous because they could contain malware such as a virus or Trojan horse. Therefore, you should confirm with the sender that he or she is in fact the sender and that the attachment is safe to open.

How to Avoid Dangerous E-Mail

There are several ways to protect yourself from dangerous e-mail.

E-MAIL FILTERS   Antimalware software provided by developers such as McAfee, Symantec, and Panda uses e-mail filters to identify malware. An e-mail filter is designed to identify, quarantine, and delete malware and spam. This task is accomplished when the software identifies the e-mail as potentially harmful. The software will quarantine the e-mail for your review later. If it is in fact determined to be harmful, it can be deleted.

DELETION The best policy for handling dangerous e-mail is to delete it. Do not get angry and reply to it. In most cases you are communicating not with a person but with a computer. Your reply will only serve to notify the computer that you are a viable e-mail address to which it can send more spam and malware.

DISCRETION Be careful who you give your e-mail address to. It is best to have at least three types of e-mail addresses. The first is your most private; it is reserved for friends and private communication. The second is for general communication with business associates and the general public in cases where you use your true identity. The third is your alias. It is used for communication with marketing groups, for making anonymous comments, or in situations where you want your identity to remain unknown.

As valuable as e-mail can be, it can also be a way for malware to enter your computer and cause damage. Do not use e-mail on your trading computer! Use e-mail only on your your backup and operations computer and your home computer. See Operations Trap 2: Avoid Malware or Get Sick Quick.

Trick 1

Back Up or Find Your Back Up against the Wall

Minimum Activity   0   1   2   3   4   5   6   7   8   Maximum Activity

Here are the top 10 reasons to back up your computer system daily:

1. The hard drive eventually will fail. Be prepared!
2. There may be accidental deletion of trade-related data.
3. Sudden power outages may damage data.
4. Power surges may damage the data on the hard drive.
5. E-mail viruses may damage data.
6. Malfunction of software could damage data.
7. Accidents such as the spilling of a drink on the computer could damage it permanently.
8. Hackers could steal your data.
9. Failure to maintain the computer properly eventually will damage data.
10. My dog ate my computer.

The problems identified here can be avoided if you implement a sound backup procedure.

The Paranoid Backup Rule

Although this level of backup is not always practical, it is important to back up your data regularly to avoid a catastrophe. At the least, back up daily to capture a daily active trading session.

Backup procedures ensure that data and application software are copied regularly and securely to protect against the loss of data or software. In the case of a disaster recovery from an emergency, it is a relief to know that you can recover and restore your active trading computer.

Backup Procedure

DATA IDENTIFICATION   Identify the important data in your computer to back up. These are the data that you will need to restore your trading computer totally. When in doubt, back it up.

BACKUP SOFTWARE APPLICATIONS   Backup software applications can be purchased to back up your data. Ironically, this software needs to be present and usable on the damaged hard disk to restore data properly. To avoid this problem, the backup software should be backed up on the same CD or DVD as the data to facilitate a complete system restoration. However, because of limited backup disk space, there may not be enough storage space for both. Therefore, it is best to back up data to a CD or DVD to make the restoration process independent of a software application.

CD/DVD BACKUP   You can use the CD or DVD read-write drive on your computer to back up data. If you do not have such a drive installed, you can purchase a CD or DVD read-write (RW) drive and plug into the computer's USB port. A CD RW can write approximately 700 MB to a single disk, and a DVD RW can write approximately 5 gigabytes to a DVD disk. Disk-writing capacity is becoming larger with new manufacturing techniques. CD or DVD media can be purchased at an office supply store.

Use the CD or DVD writing ("burning") software installed on your computer to back up data to the CD or DVD RW media. If you do not have this software, you can find free sources by searching the Web, using the search term "free CD DVD burning software." The backup CD or DVD also can be used to copy data to your backup and operations computer as well as to create a permanent record to be stored. Do not store the backup CD or DVD in the same physical location as your computers, to avoid total destruction of your data in case of a disaster.

LABEL THE BACKUP MEDIA   Label your backup CD or DVD with a meaningful name and notes. Imagine that you will be reading these notes a year from now. Will they be understandable? You will need them to be at that time.

DATA RESTORATION AND DISASTER RECOVERY   Here is the basic recovery procedure:

1. Have your new hard drive installed and made ready for use by a professional computer service.
2. Reload all system software, such as the Microsoft Windows operating system, using the original source.
3. Reload all software application software such as active trading software, using the original source.
4. Reload all data from the backup CD or DVD. This is accomplished by using Windows Explorer to copy files from the CD or DVD drive to the new hard drive. Selected files or all files can be copied by "dragging and dropping" the files to be copied from the CD/DVD to the new hard disk. It is best to practice a total data restoration to verify periodically that in fact you can recover from a disaster.

Note: If you are in doubt about how to restore data or recover from a disaster, contact a computer professional.

Back up like there is no tomorrow! There may not be!

Trick 2

E-Mail Client or Webmail? With Both, You Get Eggroll

Minimum
Activity 0 1 2 3 4 5 6 7 8
Maximum
Activity

As e-mail becomes entrenched as a form of electronic written communication, active traders need to be aware of various types of e-mail solutions and their features. What is the best form of e-mail to use? Let's explore the advantages and disadvantages of client and Web-based e-mail.

An active trader should have at least three types of e-mail addresses to serve different purposes.

Private E-Mail

A private e-mail address is reserved for communication with friends and for private communication. An e-mail client is best suited for this type of communication because it permits maximum control over the e-mails sent and received and their management. Private e-mail can utilize encryption such as Pretty Good Privacy (PGP) to prevent anyone from reading it except you and the intended recipient. Be careful who you give this e-mail address to. See the e-mail client description below.

General E-Mail

A general e-mail address is best suited for communication with business associates and the general public. A general e-mail address can have a client or Webmail orientation, depending on how much control you wish to have over the e-mail. See the Webmail description below.

Alias E-Mail

An alias e-mail address is used for communication with marketing and sales groups, anonymous contact, or any situation where you want your identity to remain unknown. It is best to use Webmail for this purpose because it reduces the ability to trace who actually owns the account.

E-Mail Client

An e-mail client is a software application, such as Microsoft Outlook or Eudora, installed on your computer. It is used to prepare, edit, send, and receive e-mail. The client permits you to have the most control over e-mail and supports the major communication protocols, such as POP3, IMAP, SMTP, and MIME, for detailed processing of e-mail stored on your ISP server computer.

E-mail clients include the following:

- Outlook
- Eudora
- Thunderbird

Note: To stay current on this topic, search the Web, using the search term "e-mail client."

ADVANTAGES

- Full word processor capability featuring a robust group of editing and e-mail processing features such as Hypertext Markup Language (HTML) that give you total control of how the text is displayed using features such bold, color, and font size.
- Control over the ISP e-mail host server computer enables the user to store e-mail on the ISP server.
- Support for "plug-in" software such as encryption for secreting e-mail messages, antimalware to detect viruses, and e-mail databases.
- Ability to process multiple e-mail accounts simultaneously.

DISADVANTAGES

- The client must be purchased.
- There is a longer learning curve to master its use.
- Messages have to be uploaded and downloaded from the Internet.
- There is a limited number of e-mail boxes per purchased e-mail account.

Web-Based E-Mail

Webmail is free a Web-based application that allows the user to read and write e-mail by using a Web browser interface. Webmail usually is offered as a free service by companies such as Yahoo, Google, and Netscape in exchange for permission to market products and services to the user. It offers basic e-mail functionality for preparing, sending, and receiving e-mails. It usually does not support the complete e-mail communication protocol standards.

Webmail service providers include the following:

- Gmail.com
- Hotmail.com
- Netscape.com
- Yahoo.com

Note: To stay current on this topic, search the Web, using the search term "Webmail" for more Webmail sources.

ADVANTAGES

- Webmail is free.
- E-mail can be sent and received from virtually anywhere because it is not installed on a specific computer, as with an e-mail client. Because it is Web-based, it can be accessed from any computer connected to the Web.
- Messages do not have to be uploaded and downloaded using the Internet.
- It is possible to sign up anonymously for an unlimited number of free Webmail addresses.
- Webmail addresses can be set up and discarded quickly.
- It permits user anonymity.

DISADVANTAGES

- The user must be connected actively to the Web to write and read e-mail.
- Webmail services offer limited e-mail storage capacity.
- There are advertisements.
- Webmail accounts receive more spam.
- The length of e-mail message is usually limited.
- There is limited control over the editing, processing, and storage of e-mail.

The best e-mail solution for the active trader is a hybrid of e-mail client and Webmail to address the challenges of communicating with different types of people for different purposes.

Trick 3

There Are Two Ears on That Mouse

Minimum  Maximum
Activity 0   1   2   3   4   5   6   7   8 Activity

Did you ever notice that your PC mouse has two buttons on it? Most people are familiar with double clicking the left mouse button to control software application functions such as opening and closing windows, launching programs, and highlighting text. However, there is an equally powerful function in the right button.

An active trader should be aware of the right button on the mouse because it often is used to perform specific functions that are unavailable with the left button. The right button function is controlled by the software application. For instance, in Microsoft (MS) Word, when you left click on the menu, a drop-down menu appears with a variety of choices, such as open, close, and save. However, if you right click on the same menu choice, you will see a completely different group of choices to control more menu choices, such as standard, formatting, and autotext. Further, right clicking on the document itself will display the most common choices from the menu.

The right click feature is very powerful in Internet Explorer. For instance, left clicking on a menu choice will control the basic functions available on the menu, such as the "Back" button, which causes the browser to load the previous Web page. However, if you right click on the same button, it will display the names of the most recent Web site home pages visited. In addition, right clicking on the menu area will provide new configurable menu features. However, in contrast, right clicking on the Web page itself will offer another menu featuring open, save target, print target and so on, associated with graphics or Web page addresses.

Always be aware of the right button, especially in trading software applications, because there may be new and more powerful commands for trading. Be curious and experiment with the right click feature. The right mouse button will open a completely new set of useful commands for the active trader, permitting you to accomplish new tricks of the trade.

Trap 1

Get Out of the Dark

Minimum Activity 0 1 2 3 4 5 6 7 8 Maximum Activity

Picture the scene. The active trader is trading away, almost ready to execute the trade, and then *boom!* The power goes off, and the trader is sitting in the dark in silence. What happened? In this situation, you better have a plan B to execute.

The Solution

Get an uninterruptible power supply (UPS). A UPS provides electrical power to the computer from an internal battery. The UPS switches on immediately when a power failure occurs so that the supply of electrical power is continued. UPS devices are taken seriously and used in facilities where it is absolutely necessary to maintain the continuity of power. As an active trader, you warrant such continuity. Further, if the power fails during the saving of data, you could lose the data.

Even a power interruption a millisecond long can cause severe problems. The longer the interruption, the more trouble. According to an IBM study, a computer could have up to 120 possible power problems per month. "Power failures or electrical surges account for 45 percent of all data loss," according to *Contingency Planning* magazine. These conditions can be prevented by using a highly rated UPS with the appropriate configuration to meet the needs of your computer and equipment. This source of clean power also will correct for electrical sags, brownouts, spikes, surges, and noise.

It is best to present your computer system configuration to a reputable UPS supplier to assure a match between your needs and UPS capacity. Here are some general terms to be aware of when selecting a UPS:

VA. Voltage amperes, a measure of the power load a UPS can support.

Power factor. The ratio of power to apparent load.

Run time. The length of time a UPS can provide its battery power.

Surge protection. The measurement, in amperes, of how big a surge the UPS can handle.

If you are serious about having a solid plan B during a power failure, you also should consider having access to a full-service broker as a backup if all else fails. Have the contact information written down on paper. Include the phone number, fax number, and address in case you have to visit the broker in person. What a novel thought.

Trap 2

Avoid Malware or Get Sick Quick

Minimum Activity 0 1 2 3 4 5 6 7 8 Maximum Activity

According to www.appriver.com, "75 percent of the global Internet traffic is spam, with a growth rate of 20 percent per year." A large portion of this spam contains a more dangerous element known as malware. Malware can be a computer virus, a worm, a Trojan horse, or any other computer program whose purpose is to cause problems on your computer. To an active trader, computer malware can be fatal to operating a computer for trading.

Malware can be divided in the following basic categories.

Viruses

A virus is a small computer program written for the sole purpose of damaging software, telecommunications, equipment, and sometimes computer hardware. It is called a virus because it simulates the mechanism used by a biological virus to embed itself, in this case getting into software and replicating itself throughout the software environment as well as other computers connected by networks. Viruses can cause severe damage to software applications and data files.

Worms

Similar to viruses, worms spread by duplicating themselves throughout the computing environment, but without embedding

139

themselves in the software application. Worms are single programs and can cause severe damage to software applications and data files.

Trojan Horses

A Trojan horse is a software program that duplicates itself under the guise of a known software application or data file. It tricks the computer's operating system into installing itself on the computer because its name is recognized as a legitimate software program such as the Microsoft "Word.exe" file. Trojan horses come in many disguises, such as a graphic, a screen saver, and an e-mail attachment. A Trojan horse also can be downloaded from the Internet or a Web site. After a computer user opens a Trojan horse, it installs itself on the computer and will not appear to do any immediate damage. However, eventually it will take over the various software applications, and it will become obvious that your computer software is not working correctly.

Antimalware Software

Malware is serious and dangerous, and you should do everything possible to reduce your exposure to it. The consequences of using damaged trading software are fatal to your trades. There are numerous providers of antimalware software, and conducting a Web search will inform you about them.

Several popular providers are:

McAfee: www.macafee.com
Symantec: www.symantec.com
Panda: www.pandachallenge.com

However, as new malware is developed, it is necessary to know how to stop it. Antimalware should be set up to monitor your computing environment constantly for potential problems and immediately stop and destroy a threat. The antimalware also should have an updating feature, automatically checking for updates to address new threats. Your antimalware software also should perform scheduled scanning of your complete computing environment for the presence of threats.

What are the symptoms of an infected computer? Data files cannot be found. Software programs do not work the way they did before. Graphics appear on the screen that have nothing to do with the software application. The most common trademark of an infection is that your computing environment has changed without your knowledge.

The most effective way to control malware is to prevent it from infecting your computer. However, if your computer becomes infected, do not panic. It is almost impossible to remove malware surgically because the computing environment is very complex. The best solution is to assemble all your application software, all the data that you so diligently backed up, and the operating system software. Format the hard drive and then reload the operating system, application software, and data files in that order. If this process seems daunting, there are companies that can perform this task for you.

Be prepared for malware to strike. Create a "disaster recovery" plan and describe in the plan what is needed to recover from any type of disaster. Let's hope you will not have to use it.

To stay current on this topic, search the Web using the search term "stop computer virus."

Trap 3

E-Mail Can Sink Your Trading

Minimum
Activity 0   1   2   3   4   5   6   7   8 Maximum
Activity

In 2002, eight U.S. brokerages were fined a total of $8 million for failing to adhere to proper e-mail guidelines under SEC rules. What does this mean to an active trader? Everything!

Criminal activity affecting Wall Street is a testimony to the fact that the mishandling of electronic documents is treated very seriously. In the case of Arthur Andersen, deletion of e-mail led to the company's downfall. It is important for active traders to take responsibility for what they communicate, and *not* having an e-mail policy in place can have severe consequences.

Be aware of *what* you put into an e-mail. It cannot be unsent and may be around forever!

Your E-Mail Policies

Here are some of the topics to consider when you are formulating your e-mail policies:

ILLEGAL USE OF E-MAIL   E-mail may seem to be a less effective form of legal communication compared with other forms of written communication. However, the same laws apply.

The following are examples of illegal use of e-mail:

- Sending an unsolicited e-mail
- Forging an e-mail

- Forwarding confidential information
- Sending an e-mail containing defamatory, offensive, racist, or obscene remarks
- Forwarding e-mail with any of these characteristics
- Forwarding e-mail without permission
- Knowingly sending an e-mail attachment that contains malware

E-MAIL ETIQUETTE   Here are tips to keep in mind:

- Use a formal style in communicating with new contacts.
- Use a spell checker in all e-mails to avoid making stupid mistakes.
- Write logically structured e-mails and use descriptive terms to communicate your intent.
- Do not send attachments that are unnecessary.
- Never write using all capital letters.
- If you forward mail, describe where the e-mail came from and why you are forwarding it.
- Do not send confidential information.
- Do not overuse the "important" designation.
- Never send user IDs or passwords or any other confidential account information.
- Write an e-mail disclaimer and attach it to all your e-mails as a signatory file. Compose a disclaimer that states that your e-mail is confidential and that it is intended for use by the intended recipient only.
- Back up your e-mails.

See Operation's Trick 1: Back Up or Find Your Back Up against the Wall. E-mail for the active trader is a double-edged sword. Be careful how and where you use it.

Software

Executing the Trade without Killing It

Minimum Activity   0   1   2   3   4   5   6   7   8   Maximum Activity

Active traders have two basic choices for trading online:

Trading software companies
Online brokers

Trading Software Companies

Trading software companies offer a dedicated method for active traders to contact their brokers and are the most effective when time is crucial in making a trade. Their software installs on the active trader's computer and provides a dedicated environment to analyze the markets and a direct communication link from the trader's computer to their "trade server." A trade server is a computer dedicated to accepting and processing a trade on behalf of the active trader. The active trader also is provided a similar direct access to the "quote server," a computer that provides the latest real-time market quotes. Most of these trading software companies are introducing brokers (IBs) and provide direct access to the broker for the execution of a trade. The following is a partial list of trading software companies. To find additional trading software companies, search the Web using the term "active trader broker."

www.tradeportal.com
www.efloortrade.com
www.esignal.com
www.tradestation.com
www.cybertrader.com
www.qcharts.com

Online Brokers

Online brokers offer a link with reduced speed and quality communications to their trade server and quote server because they are accessed by an active trader using a Web browser such as Internet Explorer (IE) and the Internet. Online brokers are most effective for an active trader in scenarios where time is not crucial to the trade. Their services are accessible from the active trader's computer over the Internet to the broker. The major time delay occurs when the browser connects to the broker's trade server and quote server via the Web. The Web browser is subject to more restrictions, such as Internet traffic, than is a direct connection used by trading software companies. Most of these companies are introducing brokers and may cause further delays in executing a trade to the exchange. The following is a partial list of online brokers. To find additional online brokers, search the Web, using the term "active trader online broker."

www.schwab.com
www.etrade.com
www.ameritrade.com
www.fidelity.com

To evaluate both trading methods, an active trader should set up an evaluation checklist for both trading environments in order to compare their value and performance. The evaluation checklist should include at least the following topics:

1. *Security*. What safeguards are in place to protect your trading environment, personal information, and financial assets?
2. *Security updates*. What are the ongoing security update measures?
3. *User ID and passwords*. How do they control the issuance and use of user IDs and passwords?
4. *Firewall*. What protection is offered by the trading platform firewall?
5. *Monitoring your account*. How are cookies used to monitor your trading activity? What is the company's cookie policy?
6. *Encryption*. What type of encryption is used? How does it compare to current encryption standards?
7. *Secure Socket Layer (SSL)*. Do they use SSL for online security? SSL is crucial to online security.
8. *Privacy*. What is their privacy policy?
9. *Identity theft*. How is identity theft prevented?
10. *Malware*. How is malware such as worms, Trojan horses, and scripts blocked in the telecommunication connection between the active trader and the broker?

Software Solutions

The following is a brief overview of selected active trader online solutions provided by various trading software companies and online brokers. This overview is by no means comprehensive or complete. It is meant to introduce active traders to online trading solutions. To evaluate these and other active trading solutions more fully, conduct a personal and more extensive search of what is currently available for online trading.

Tip 1

The Internet Is Your Friend

Minimum  Maximum
Activity 0 1 2 3 4 5 6 7 8 Activity

The Internet is a worldwide network of telecommunication connections among millions of computers. The Internet is based on a telecommunications system designed by DARPA for the U.S. military in the 1960s. It was designed to survive a nuclear attack and uses a decentralized approach to communicating between computers, permitting it to reroute communications if it encounters an impasse. It is publicly accessible worldwide and consists of a complex system of interconnected computer servers that transmit information via a "packet switch" standard known as the Internet Protocol (IP). It is used by millions of commercial, academic, domestic, and governmental entities. The Internet serves to transmit information and services, such as e-mail, instant messaging, and chat, and ultimately serves as the foundation for the World Wide Web.

The World Wide Web

The Web was conceived by Berners-Lee at CERN, a Swiss nuclear physics research laboratory. He wrote a software application that would permit the transmission of graphic files, or "Web pages," between computers connected by the Internet. The first successful transmission was on Christmas Day, 1990, and his colleagues at CERN started using the application to transfer information about nuclear physics. In 1993, "Web browsers" such as Mosaic replaced Berners-Lee's program. Since then, the Web has served as one of the most powerful forms of communication between people worldwide.

Active Trading and the Web

The Web permits an individual to be an active trader by offering unprecedented access to research, company information, and real-time news for making an informed trade. Active traders rely heavily on the Internet and the Web to contact trading software or online brokers to process their trades.

Tip 2

Choose a Good ISP or Lose Your Choice

Minimum Activity  Maximum Activity

0   1   2   3   4   5   6   7   8

Before choosing an ISP, evaluate your active trading environment needs. Once they are identified, it is easier to make a choice. It is important to consider the following factors when evaluating an ISP:

- *Technical support.* Technical support is very important. However, it is necessary to determine first how much support you will need. ISPs offer different levels of support, such as support for a certain number of hours a day; others offer 24-hour access to a live person 365 days a year at any hour. As an active trader, you are advised to use an ISP with a $24 \times 7 \times 365$ live support service. However, note the fees charged for such service and make sure the support phone number is toll-free and has an emergency backup number.
- *Price.* This is not the place to shop for a bargain. As an active trader, it is important for you to know what level of support you need in making the connection to your broker.
- *Service contract.* What is the total group of services offered by the ISP? It pays to shop around and get the best contract to meet your needs in a total package. Often ISP contracts are for at least one year, especially a T-1 line and satellite. However, broadband cable and DSL contracts are monthly.
- *Frequency of use.* How often do you use the Internet to trade? Daily, weekly, or monthly? Most ISPs charge a flat monthly

rate or charge for the amount of time you spend online per hour or day. Some ISPs offer a choice between these two basic options. If you are using the Internet for active trading and know you will be spending a lot of time on it every day, a monthly structure would make the most sense. If you know you will be online only periodically, the hourly option would be advisable.

- *Time of use.* The time of the day you use the Internet affects your rate. Most ISPs charge higher rates during peak hours (9 a.m. to 5 p.m.). Typically, the off-peak hours after 5 p.m. are less expensive.
- *Spam and viruses.* Choose an ISP with a strong antispam and antivirus policy. In addition, the ISP should offer a spam and virus filtering service to protect you from damage to your trading system.
- *Availability of a Web site.* ISPs offer customers a limited amount of Web space as an add-on to the service or as part of the package. If you plan to have a Web site, this added service is a consideration in the overall ISP package.

Note: To stay current on this topic, search the Web using the search term "ISP high speed."

Tip 3

The Need for Connection Speed

Minimum Activity 0 1 2 3 4 5 6 7 8 Maximum Activity

The other half of the speed equation for active trading is the connection speed from your computer to your broker's computer. The connection speed is crucial in placing your trades at the right moment and as quickly as possible. The main rule is that faster is better. However, do not overlook the obvious. If you want your order to be filled immediately at the Chicago Mercantile Exchange, trade from downtown Chicago, not from Honolulu, Hawaii. Do not even think about a dial-up connection for active trading except as an emergency backup connection.

There are four major ways to reach the Internet: satellite, T1, broadband cable, and DSL. Internet Service Providers are companies that provide access to the Internet. ISPs offer connection to the Internet in the following major formats.

Satellite

Satellite Internet service should be used only if it is not possible to connect to the Internet using T1, cable, or DSL. In a two-way satellite connection, the uplink data transmission to the satellite is at a slower speed than the downlink. The receiving antenna dish, which is approximately two feet by three feet, transmits and receives satellite signals. The uplink speeds are nominally 50 to 150 kilobits per second (Kbps). The downlink speeds are from 150 to

1,200 Kbps, depending on Internet traffic, the capacity of the server, and the sizes of data files. Satellite Internet systems are quite impressive, but they tend to be the most expensive. Also, what do you do if there is a problem with the satellite? Wait!

T1

A T1 Internet connection supports data rates of 1.544 Mbits per second. T1 lines consist of 24 individual channels; each channel supports 64 Kbits per second and can be set up to carry voice or data traffic. Most phone companies offer individual channels known as fractional T1s. T1 lines are the most common for connecting to the Internet at high speeds, and the T1 line is actually a fraction of the higher-speed Internet T3 backbone used for global Internet traffic.

Broadband Cable

A broadband Internet connection operates over cable TV coaxial lines. Cable Internet uses a dedicated TV channel space for data transmission. Some of the channel space is used for downstream transmission, and some for upstream transmission. Because the coaxial cable provides a much greater bandwidth than do telephone lines, a cable modem is necessary to achieve fast access to the Internet. Typical cable speeds are 1.5 Mbps or higher.

DSL

DSL uses existing copper telephone wires to access the Internet. It uses amplifiers to boost the signal every mile. Therefore, DSL connections are subject to performance problems if an amplifier fails.

DSL is often less expensive than T1 and broadband cable, but the price of performance should be considered. DSL should be considered only if T1 and broadband cable are not available.

Backup Connection

It is a good idea to have an Internet backup for your primary Internet connection. Your backup could be a duplicate of your primary Internet connection with another ISP or a viable alternative, as described above. Of course, always be prepared to call your broker on the phone if the Internet connection fails.

Tip 4

Browsing for Browsers

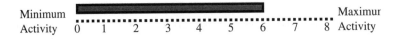

| Minimum Activity | 0 | 1 | 2 | 3 | 4 | 5 | 6 | 7 | 8 | Maximur Activity |

An active trader can use a variety of resources on the Web, including a Web browser, to leverage the quality of his or her research. The Web browsers discussed below offer unique approaches to searching, and each has its own strengths and weaknesses.

Internet Explorer

Internet Explorer (IE) by Microsoft is available at www. microsoft.com. To date, IE is the most popular Web browser. It is bundled with the Windows operating system, and a majority of trade-related Web sites recommend its use. Online brokers such as Charles Schwab utilize IE Active X to control page display. IE has become the de facto standard supported by most online brokers. However, that standard has a problem: IE is the number one browser for hackers to attack by exploiting its weaknesses with malware such as viruses. As a result, IE is under continuous attack. Microsoft is constantly improving the security and perform- ance of IE and addressing these problems actively, but it is a con- stant war between Microsoft and the hackers. It is important to be diligent by downloading the latest version of IE and adjusting the security settings appropriately to provide a secure platform for active trading.

Firefox

Firefox by Mozilla is available at www.mozilla.org. Firefox is gaining in popularity and offers a faster method for browsing the Web in comparison to IE. Firefox has the same basic features as IE, but it is not subject to all the malware written to attack IE. The problem with Firefox is that it will not always display Web site pages that are dedicated to use IE correctly. Firefox is enhanced continuously by a large community of volunteer coders. When vulnerability is discovered, it is corrected immediately, and the update is made available for free for all users. This unique community support enables Firefox to adapt very quickly to fix problems and avoid the update delays often associated with IE. In conclusion, Firefox is best suited for researching the Web for information and avoiding malware. However, until it is embraced more fully by online brokers, it will be difficult for active traders to rely on it for making trades.

Grokker

Grokker by Groxis Inc. is available at www.grokker.com. The Grokker Web browser interface produces a one-page display of all the results located in a keyword search. All the information is displayed completely on one page in the form of different colored geometric shapes: circles, squares, and triangles. This unique feature permits active traders to see a visual map of all information and results. Typical Web browsers display consecutive pages of text, resulting in page after page of results. The Grokker display features a large colored circle that contains a different colored square that contains a different colored triangle. Each geometric shape is labeled to produce a "map" of search results that can be saved for later reference. Grokker features the ability to click on a labeled circle and "drill down" further into more colored and labeled circles, squares, and triangles. The final display features the actual Web page of information containing the keywords of the search. This research display feature is remarkable and very useful in displaying the complete universe of information found in a keyword search and the relationship of the keywords. Grokker uses a variety of search engines, such as Google and Yahoo, to drive the Web search.

SpeedResearch

The SpeedResearch browser is available at www.speedresearch.com. The SpeedResearch browser was created specifically for researching trade-related information by active traders. SpeedResearch is a fee-based browser that is designed to be more efficient in working with stock research, quoting, and charting Web sites. It also features built-in dynamic links to access popular stock data Web sites and integrate the data into your portfolio. Another useful feature permits a trader to access Microsoft Word and Excel applications to import historical data and manage documents for quoting, charting, and further research.

To utilize the Web adequately for active trading and research, an active trader should use a variety of Web browsers that reflect his or her unique needs and trading strategy. Further information can be gained by searching the Web using the search term "Web browser active trading."

Trick 1

Bookmark That Baby

Minimum
Activity  Maximum
Activity

0   1   2   3   4   5   6   7   8

During the search for information relevant to a trade, an active trader needs to store the exact Web site page containing information of interest. Most people are familiar with using Microsoft Internet Explorer to bookmark a Web page. This is accomplished by clicking on the IE menu choice "Favorites" and then "Add to Favorites" and then "OK." However, this will save the Web page to your favorites list, but after saving thousands of Web pages, how do you find what you want? Remember, the trick is to be organized; that is half the battle.

By creating a new favorites folder, you can save Web pages in a relevant location that allows later retrieval. This task is accomplished easily by clicking the IE favorites menu and then chosing "Organize Favorites." Click "Create Folder," type in the folder name, and then click "Close." The next time you wish to save a Web page to that new folder, click on "Favorites" and "Add to Favorites" and then "Create In." Highlight the folder name and then click "OK." You are done.

If the new folder becomes too big, create a subfolder within the folder. This follows a method similar to the one used to create file folders in Windows Explorer. Similarly, IE also permits you to "Rename," "Move to Folder," and "Delete" a Web page.

To retrieve a Web page, click "Favorites" and "File Folder," highlight the Web page name, and click once to open the Web page.

Web site addresses are subject to change. Be sure to check your bookmarks periodically to make sure they are valid. If a Web site bookmark is no longer valid, return to the original Web site and search the site for words relevant to the original bookmark subject matter. If the Web site has disappeared completely, use a search engine such as Google to find out where it might be located.

Remember, if you can't find it, you have lost it!

Trick 2

Search the Web They Weave

Minimum
Activity

0   1   2   3   4   5   6   7   8
Maximum
Activity

The Web is here to stay, and you are most likely a part of it. Try going to www.google.com or www.yahoo.com and typing in your name. Are you there? The practice of going to a library and taking out a book for current information may be a lost art. Information is being transferred to the Web by the second, and finding information in a timely manner requires a Web search. This is especially true for active traders searching for information about their trades.

How does an active trader find search engines relevant to her or his interests? The trick is to search the Web using the terms "search engine" and "active trader." The result of this search will direct you to many search engines that have vast amounts of information for active traders.

Additional Web sites for research by an active trader can be found at the following Web addresses:

Company Research

www.finance.yahoo.com
www.hoovers.com
www.smallbusiness.dnb.com
www.corporateinformation.com
www.edgar-online.com
www.lexis-nexis.com
www.thomasregister.com

Business News

www.news.com
www.multexinvestors.com
www.newsalert.com

Futures Research

www.xpresstrade.com
www.futuresource.com

Stock Research

www.bloomberg.com
www.dailystocks.com

Note: This list of Web sites is by no means comprehensive or complete and is subject to change over time. This is only a starting point.

Trick 3

Save to the Web

Minimum Activity 0 1 2 3 4 5 6 7 8 Maximum Activity

You would think that with the millions of computer servers connected to the Internet, surely there would be some way to utilize them to store your data. Your prayers have been answered! One cost-free method of backing up your data is to e-mail your data files as attachments to your Webmail account.

This is easily accomplished by first creating a Webmail account at a Web site such as www.yahoo.com, www.gmail.com, or www. hotmail.com. At the Webmail host, create an e-mail message and attach the files on your computer to be backed up to the e-mail message. Then send the e-mail to your Webmail address. This will back up your data files on the Webmail host and permit you to access them at any time and from any location with Web access. Most Webmail hosts permit you to attach up to 5 MB of data per e-mail address. Many Webmail hosts provide up to 1 GB of total storage for free, to be used in any way, such as storage of e-mail, data files, video and audio files, and so on.

The value of this process to an active trader is that it is a simple and fast way to back up a file indefinitely at your Webmail account. Further, you can e-mail the attached file to another e-mail address, such as that of a fellow trader, by entering that person's e-mail address in the "cc:" header. This process can send attachments up to 5 MB in size and can be repeated until you reach the capacity of your e-mail box.

But wait a minute. How do you retrieve the file? Go to your Webmail "in box" and open the e-mail with the attached file of interest. Click on the attached filename, and the file will be opened automatically by the software application that created it, such as Microsoft Word. This is a quick method to back up data files, and you cannot beat the price—Free! *Caution*: Both Google and Yahoo scan e-mail for marketing purposes.

Trick 4

Let the Information Find You

Minimum
Activity  Maximum
Activity

A portion of any active trader's time is spent researching trade-related information on stocks, bonds, and options to determine the best performance value. The majority of this research time is spent actively searching the Web. Why not let this type of information find you?

There are a variety of electronic "news clipping" services that will register your interests in the form of keywords of interest to you. For instance, if you are interested in monitoring IBM's stock performance, it is possible to create a search profile using the keyword "IBM" and select information categories such as news, stock performance, and analyst reviews that will be sent to your e-mail box on a periodic basis.

The following is a brief list of fee-based news clipping services:

www.businesswire.com
www.dowjones.com
www.hoovers.com
www.investors.com
www.spyonit.com
www.webclipping.com
www.worldnews.com
www.google.com

Note: Additional information about this type of service can be found by searching the Web using the keywords: electronic news clipping.

News Groups

Another way to be informed in a timely manner about active traders' interests is to subscribe to news groups. News groups were created to inform people with a common interest in a specific subject. To receive information from a specific news group, it is necessary to visit the news group's Web page and subscribe by providing your e-mail address. News groups are usually free, and active traders can benefit from them by receiving e-mail alerts about news, getting, subscribers' opinions, and having an interactive dialogue with other subscribers.

Google.com

To subscribe to Google news groups, use Google to search for "active trader." Then click on "Groups." Subscribe with your e-mail address. Google has a free news clipping service called "News Alerts." At the Google home page, click on "More" and choose "News Alerts."

Yahoo.com

Yahoo offers Yahoo Groups to provide information to subscribers. For more information on Yahoo Groups, visit Yahoo.com and click on "Groups." Enter the keywords "Active Trader" to locate specific groups of interest and subscribe with your e-mail address. Now you can spend your time more effectively by reading e-mail information related directly to your interests and analyzing that information to make wise trades. For more information on this topic, search the Web using the keywords "active trader newsgroup."

Trick 5

Tidbits

WEB ADDRESS   Often you do not have to use "http://www." in a Web address. Simply type in the main portion of the Uniform Resource Locator (URL) Web address. For instance, in searching for the URL http://www.yahoo.com, simply use yahoo.com.

PRINT A WEB PAGE   A Web page can be printed by choosing "File" and "Print." Normally, the Web page will print to your printer. However, if you have "Fax" as your selected printer, it will convert the Web page to a fax, permitting you to fax the Web page.

SEND A WEB PAGE   A Web page can be sent to someone in several ways by e-mail. Use menu choice "File" and "Send." Choose "Page by e-mail" to send the Web page in an e-mail or "Link by e-mail" to send the Web page URL link.

PROGRESSIVELY SAVE SEARCHES   Use the browser to search for primary keywords first. After the search is displayed, you can save the search results by clicking "Add to Favorites" and save the material to the appropriate file folder. This permits you to add new or different keywords progressively and save the searches.

FIND A WORD ON A WEB PAGE   Instead of reading a complete Web page to find what you want, use the main menu choice "Edit" and then "Find." Type in your keyword and click "Find Next," and you will find it automatically.

USE OF UPPERCASE LETTERS   It is very rarely necessary to use uppercase letters in Web browsing.

GRAPHIC IMAGES   When you see a graphic picture on a Web page, right click the mouse on it and you can save it, e-mail it to someone, or print it.

FONT SIZE   Having trouble reading a Web page because the text is too small? Use the menu choice "View" and change the text size to one of five sizes.

VIEWING AREA   To view more of a Web page, use the menu choice "View" to click off "Toolbars" and "Full Screen" for a maximum Web page display.

COPY AND PASTE A WEB PAGE   You can copy a complete Web page by clicking on the "Edit" menu choice and then "Select All." Click the right mouse button and choose "Copy." Selected parts of a Web page can be copied by positioning the mouse cursor at the beginning of the information to be copied. Hold down the left mouse button and drag the cursor down the Web page to highlight it. After it is highlighted, click on the right mouse button and select "Copy." Now you can paste the Web page into any software application, such as Word, Excel, or Paint.

Trap 1

Who Is That New Me?

Minimum Activity  Maximum Activity

0   1   2   3   4   5   6   7   8

Did you ever look in the mirror and not recognize the person you saw? This is what you will be doing if your identity is stolen. There will be a new you in cyberspace with an agenda completely different from yours. If you are an active trader, your trading account could be emptied or used for bad trades, for which you would be liable.

Identity theft is the fastest-growing Internet-based crime. In 2003, losses from fraud amounted to more than $500 million. During that year the Federal Trade Commission (FTC) received over 500,000 identity theft complaints, three times the amount made in 2002. It is estimated that in 2005, one in four people was the victim of identity theft.

The most common form of identity theft occurs when someone acquires your credit card information. This is accomplished in several ways; the most common is when your credit or debit card is lost or stolen. Your liability for credit cards and debit cards is different, and you should check with your issuing bank to discover your limit of exposure. Be aware that a common method of identity theft is done at the point of transaction. The card's information can be swiped and recorded for illegal use later. Be sure to check your card usage online and your monthly statements.

The more powerful form of identity theft occurs when the criminal actually assumes your identity completely. Once someone

167

has your Social Security number, it is possible to research you on the Web to find out more about you. Ultimately, the thief assumes your identity accurately and applies for credit cards, a driver's license, bank loans, and the like, in your name. However, the contact address is the thief's, and all new credit information is sent to him or her.

Prevention of identity theft is difficult, and unfortunately, there is not a clear path to restoring your identity and credit. In most cases, it takes at least a year of your lawyer's time and several thousand dollars to restore your identity and credit rating. However, there are procedures that you can use to begin the process of restoring your good credit.

1. Contact the following major credit bureaus:

   Equifax: www.equifax.com
   Equifax Consumer Fraud Division
   PO Box 740241
   Atlanta, GA 30374-0241
   Phone: 800-525-6285

   Experian: www.experian.com
   Experian National Consumer Assistance
   PO Box 9532
   Allen, TX 75013
   Phone: 888-397-3742

   TransUnion: www.tuc.com
   TransUnion Fraud Victim Assistance Department
   PO Box 6790
   Fullerton, CA 92834-6790 Phone: 800-680-7289

   Contact the Social Security Administration at 800-269-0271.

   These bureaus are required to provide you with a free credit report in the case of identity theft. Be sure to request a report from each bureau. Each credit bureau will have advice on what to do if you are a victim of identity theft. Notify each of them to identify your credit report and tell you the extent of the damage done. Immediately put a restriction on opening new accounts in your name. Close all accounts that you did not open.

2. Make a police report about the identity theft.

Protecting Yourself Against Identity Theft

1. Avoid using public computers in airports, hotels, libraries, and restaurants because they may have been infected with "key loggers" to record personal information.
2. Check your credit regularly and get a copy of your credit report every year.
3. Check credit and debit card statements.
4. Keep your credit and debit card receipts for a year.
5. Protect your surface mailbox from tampering.
6. Buy a shredder and use it. Dumpster diving for personal information is *not* illegal.
7. Do not give out personal finance information on the phone unless you know to whom you are speaking.
8. Change your password regularly.

Active traders should be especially aware of identity theft because of the amount of personal and financial information they must register to open and operate a trading account. Constant vigilance is necessary to protect your identity on and off the Web.

Trap 2

Your Kingdom

Minimum Activity   0   1   2   3   4   5   6   7   8   Maximum Activity

The most crucial aspect of accessing an active trader account is the online user ID and password. Therefore, protecting your user ID and password is crucial to preventing misuse of your account. In the wrong hands, your trading account can be depleted of funds in seconds, and your recourse is minimal. Planning and management of your user ID and passwords is paramount.

User ID and Password Management

The user ID and password usually are provided by your broker but may be selected by you. In either case, it is *your* responsibility to control its secrecy. The trick is to have different levels of user IDs and passwords that are easy for you to remember but difficult for others to guess. To accomplish the secure management of user IDs and passwords, it is necessary to have a plan that permits you to manage their life cycle logically.

The typical life cycle of a user ID and password goes through three distinct stages.

STAGE I: USER ID AND PASSWORD ISSUANCE The user ID and password should be issued *only* to you. It is wise to change the password as soon as you receive it to guarantee that only you know what it is.

STAGE II: PASSWORD USE   Ideally, you should commit your user IDs and passwords to memory. When you use your trading account, do not write down the user ID and password on paper or mention it in any form of communication. It is best to keep a list of your current user IDs and passwords in a word-processed file for reference. This file should have a password protecting it from unauthorized access. Be sure to back up this file in several places so that you can access it when necessary. If you must keep a written list of your current user IDs and passwords, keep the list under lock and key and *not* in the same location as your trading computer.

STAGE III: UPDATING PASSWORDS   The final stage in using a user ID and password is to update them. In general, you should change your password as often as necessary on the basis of risk, perceived or actual. The higher the chance of financial loss, the higher the risk. You should consider changing your password often because it is more difficult to "hit a moving target" that is constantly changing. The frequency of updating a password is a personal choice; however, a monthly change of password is about average. In situations where you believe your password may have been compromised, it is best to set up a completely different user ID and password account to remove all doubt.

You must personally set up and manage your own security management system. It is worth it! Online security account management has different levels of passwords associated with different functions, such as Webmail, public Web sites, and bank Accounts.

The following three levels of user IDs and passwords are intended only as general guidelines for setting up user IDs and passwords:

> *Alias account user IDs and passwords.* Alias account user IDs and passwords refer to Webmail, e-mail newsletters, Web site

access, and the like. These user IDs and passwords should
not have to be changed, because there is no consequence to
their being discovered. Further, they are attached to your
online alias name and identity, not to the real you.

Private account user IDs and passwords. Private account
user IDs and passwords refer to your private e-mail
account, Web-based accounts, or any other online account
that uses your real private information. These user IDs
and passwords should be changed often, because the
consequences of their being discovered and misused could
be devastating. Private account passwords should be
changed at least every three months. The frequency of
change is personal and is based on perceived or actual
damage if they were to be discovered.

Top secret user IDs and passwords. Top secret account user
IDs and passwords refer to your online money accounts,
such as your bank account and trading account. In
addition, they encompass your personal identity accounts.
Both are extremely valuable. These user IDs and passwords
should be changed more often because the consequences of
their being discovered and misused could be devastating.
Top secret account passwords should be changed at least
once a month.

Password Creation

A secure password should include alphabetical (A–Z) and numeric
(0–9) characters as well as these special characters: $, #, @, *. It
should be at least eight characters in length and have a personal
meaning to you. However, it should not be obvious to others.

Avoid using the following:

- Your birth date or other relevant personal dates as your password
- Your address, phone number, or other personalized numbers as part of your password
- Your name or the name of people you know as part of your password
- Common names spelled forward or backward

Expert hackers and identity theft criminals utilize special software applications capable of generating all common words and permutations of your personal information very quickly and submit them to access your account automatically and continuously. With time they will succeed. Only the paranoid survive: If you are seriously paranoid about using online user IDs and passwords, do not use the computer and the Internet for active trading. Use the old-fashioned way of trading: Call your broker on the telephone!

Now a word about Lewis Carroll. He was quoted at the beginning this section. And we would like to conclude as follows:

> When you come to any passage you don't understand, *read it again*. If you *still* don't understand it, *read it again*. If you fail even after *three* readings, your brain is getting a little tired. In that case, put the book away and take to other occupations. The next day, when you come to it fresh, you very likely will find that it is *quite* easy.

Part 3

Trader's Notebook

Every trader has a binder for notes and new trading ideas. Here are some of the concepts in my binder. When you receive your free updates, you may wish to save them.

Trader's Notebook 1

Sooner or Later You Must Excel

By Mark Tinghino

Mark Tinghino has a B.A. in Philosophy from University of Illinois at Chicago and attended University of Chicago as an MA/Ph.D. candidate in South Asian Languages and Civilization. He has published several magazine and online articles on trading and teaches trading seminars at the Chicago Board of Trade and the Chicago Mercantile Exchange. He has been a trader since 1983 and a Commodity Trading Advisor since 1987. In addition to being a CTA, he is also an analyst with Worldwide Associates, LLC in Chicago.

Minimum Activity										Maximum Activity
	0	1	2	3	4	5	6	7	8	

This chapter explains how to create an Excel worksheet from a Web page. Microsoft Excel is a useful program for all sorts of quantitative analysis. It is easy for the average person to master without having to become a full-fledged computer programmer. Here are some examples that demonstrate how to use several of the features in Excel for portfolio and market price analysis.

Example 1: Stocks

In Excel, a worksheet is arranged in columns and rows; this is known as a tabular format. Each table item, called a cell, is referenced by its position, that is, its row and column. Thus, the cell in the upper left corner is in position A1.

From the Excel menu, with your mouse select Data—Import External Data—New Web Query, as shown in Figure P3-1 (A). For those who are new to the mouse, one uses the left button to make menu selections and click on Windows controls. For any of the steps below, a left mouse click is implied unless stated otherwise.

You should see a window like the one shown in Figure P3-2.

Type http://moneycentral.msn.com/detail/stock_quote? Symbol= GOOG in the address field and click the Go button. You will find

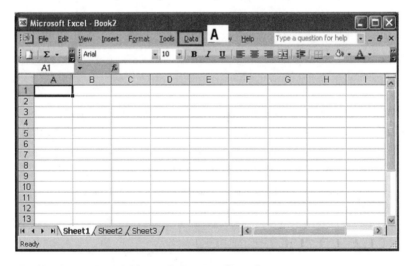

Figure P3-1   Excel Menu Selection (Data)

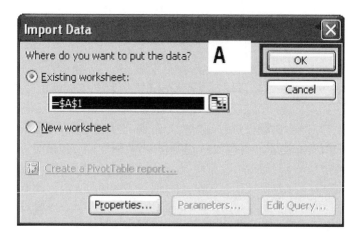

Figure P3-2   Excel Pop-up Dialog for Destination of Imported Data

a table in the center of the MSN Money Web page containing the price quotes and other statistics on Google Inc's stock. Each table on the Web page will have a black arrow in a yellow square to the left of it. Click on the black arrow in the yellow square to the left of the table header, which should show up as a blue bar with "GOOG quote" text on it. The arrow should change to a black check mark on a blue square. Then click on the Import button.

A window will prompt you to indicate where the table data will be inserted into your worksheet. It will default to wherever your mouse cursor is positioned. In this example it is in the upper left corner of the worksheet at cell A1.

Click on OK after positioning the mouse cursor on the cell in your Excel worksheet where you want the upper left corner of the table to start. You should see the worksheet fill up with values, as shown in Figure P3-3.

Now you can customize this Web query to use it with any stock symbol you wish.

Right click on any cell within the table region of your worksheet and choose Edit Query. For example, you could click on the cell A4, as shown in Figure P3-4 (A). You should see a window that looks like the one in Figure P3-4. Then click on the Save As icon to the far right of the toolbar at the top of the window, as shown in Figure P3-5 (A).

Change the Save In folder to My Documents by clicking on the My Documents icon, as shown in Figure P3-6 (A). Name the file something descriptive such as GoogleStockQuote in the File name (B) and click the Save button (C).

	A	B	C	D	E
1	GOOG quote		Real-time quotes		
2	421.18 up+21.72 +5.44%fyi				
3	fyi Volume	12.56 Mil	GOOG Intraday Chart		
4	fyi Avg Daily Volume	10.5 Mil	Intraday Chart		
5	Day's High	423.51	NASDAQ Exchange		
6	Day's Low	405.73	5d 1m 3m 1y 3y 5y 10y		
7	Open	407.38	Data Source: CSI 12:14 PM ET		
8	Previous Close	399.46	Quotes delayed 15 minutes		
9	Bid	421.08			
10	Bid Size	500			
11	Ask	421.18			
12	Ask Size	100	Current Div. Yield	NA	
13	52 Week High	475.11	Market Cap.	124.5 Bil	
14	52 Week Low	172.57	Tot. Shares Out.	295.5 Mil	
15	Instit. Ownership	51.00%	Forward P/E	67.3	
16	P/E	88.2	Sales	5.251 Bil	
17	Earnings/Share	4.53	Return on Equity	14.8	
18	Div/Share	NA	Beta	-0.07	
19					

Figure P3-3   Excel Worksheet Showing Imported Stock Price Data, Etc.

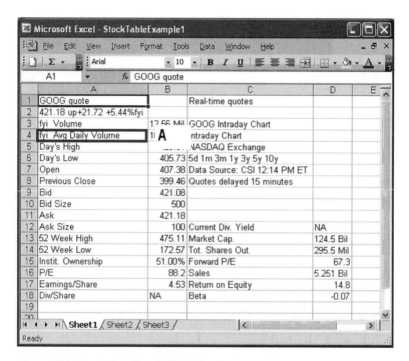

Figure P3-4   Selecting Cell A4 in the Excel Worksheet

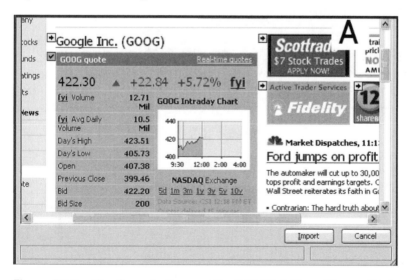

Figure P3-5   The Save As Icon on the Edit Web Query Popup Dialog

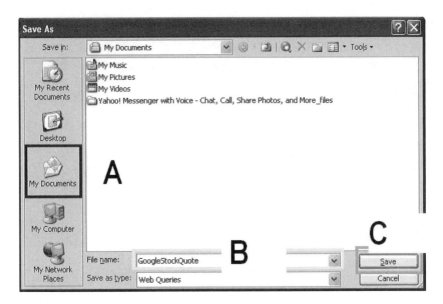

Figure P3-6   The Save As Pop-up Dialog

Next, open Notepad from your Start menu under Accessories and choose File—Open from the menu, as shown in Figure P3-7 (A). Then find your file.

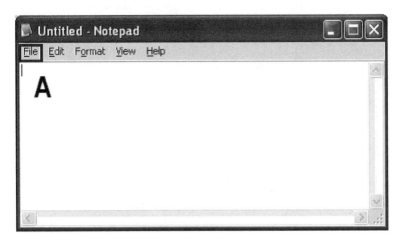

Figure P3-7   Microsoft Notepad Text Editor Software

Figure P3-8   MS Notepad Showing Contents of the Excel Web Query

The file should read something like the one shown in Figure P3-8.

Change the line that begins with http://to http://moneycentral. msn.com/detail/stock_quote?Symbol=["Symbol", "Enter Ticker Symbol"], as shown in the black rectangle in Figure P3-9. Save the file by choosing File—Save from the Notepad menu (A).

In case you have not figured out this approach, we have replaced the symbol for Google with a different parameter that will tell Excel that we need to feed information to the Web query.

Now select Sheet 2 and type CBH in cell A1. This is the stock symbol for Commerce Bancorp, as shown in Figure P3-10.

From the Excel menu, choose Data—Import External Data— Import Data. You should see a window that looks just like the one shown in Figure P3-11.

Click on the My Documents folder (highlighted in white in Figure P3-12) and find your query file. Double click on it.

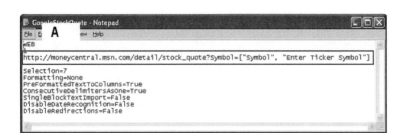

Figure P3-9   Adding the Web Site Link Prompt for the Web Query in Notepad

Then click on the Parameters button in the Import Data window, as shown in Figure P3-13 (A).

Select "Get the value from the following cell" button and then click in the white box just below it and then on cell A1 in your worksheet, as shown in Figure P3-14 (A). Click OK (B).

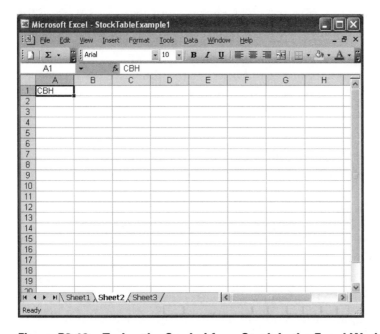

Figure P3-10   Typing the Symbol for a Stock in the Excel Worksheet

Figure P3-11   Data Source Selection Pop-up Dialog in Excel

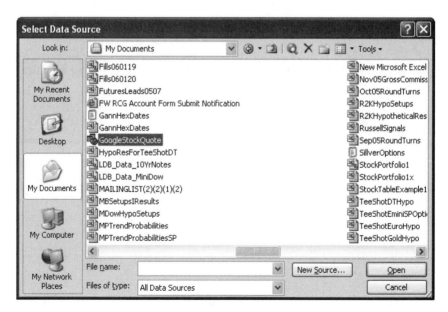

Figure P3-12   Searching for and Selecting the File for the Web Query in the My Documents Folder

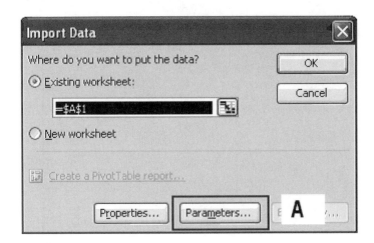

Figure P3-13   The Parameters Button in the Import Data Pop-up Dialog

You should see the worksheet fill up with the table values for Commerce Bancorp, as shown in Figure P3-15.

Now you can flag certain values, such as a price/earnings ratio that is higher than 20. Position the mouse cursor on the P/E field in Sheet 1 and choose Format—Conditional Formatting from the Excel top menu. You should see a window open like the one shown in Figure P3-16.

For Condition 1, change the drop-down list in the center to "greater than" (A) and type 20 in the text box on the right (B). Then click on the Format button (C). You should then see a window open like the one shown in Figure P3-17.

Click on the Patterns tab (A) and choose red from the color selection palette. Click OK.

If the P/E ratio for Google is higher than 20, you should see the value with a red background, as shown in Figure P3-18 (shaded cell).

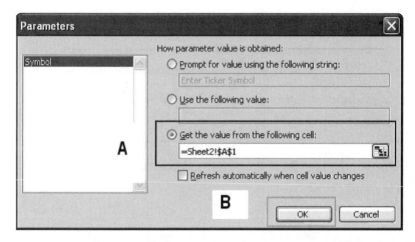

Figure P3-14   Selecting the Radio Button for Getting the Parameter Value from a Cell in the Excel Worksheet

	A	B	C	D	E
1	CBH quote		Real-time quotes		CBH
2	32.35 up+0.14 +0.43%				
3	Volume	569,500	CBH Intraday Chart		
4	Avg Daily Volume	2.178 Mil	Intraday Chart		
5	Day's High	32.57	NYSE Exchange		
6	Day's Low	32.15	5d 1m 3m 1y 3y 5y 10y		
7	fyi Open	32.21	Data Source: CSI 12:50 PM ET		
8	Previous Close	32.21	Quotes delayed 20 minutes		
9	Bid	NA			
10	Bid Size	1,800			
11	Ask	NA			
12	Ask Size	500	Current Div. Yield	1.5	
13	52 Week High	35.98	Market Cap.	5.618 Bil	
14	52 Week Low	26.87	Tot. Shares Out.	173.7 Mil	
15	Instit. Ownership	87.10%	Forward P/E	17.7	
16	fyi P/E	17.9	Sales	1.986 Bil	
17	Earnings/Share	1.8	Return on Equity	14.7	
18	fyi Div/Share	0.48	Beta	0.59	
19					

Figure P3-15   Excel Worksheet Containing Data for Commerce Bancorp

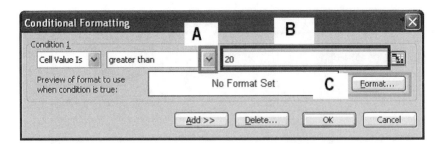

Figure P3-16   Setting up the Conditional Formatting in the Excel Pop-up Dialog

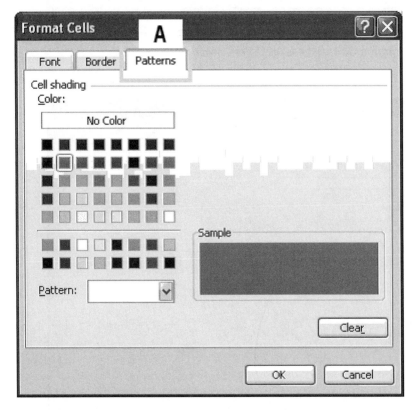

Figure P3-17   Setting the Color for the Conditional Format in the Format Cells Pop-up Dialog

Now switch to Sheet 2 and repeat the steps listed above to format the P/E ratio. Then add another condition, this time formatting the value to have a yellow background if the P/E ratio is less than 18, as shown in Figure P3-18.

If the P/E ratio for Commerce Bancorp is less than 18 at the time you are reading this, you should see the value with a yellow background, as shown in Figure P3-19 (shaded with a black border).

Now you can calculate a 52-week range that will always work correctly even if your 52-week high and low values in the table are not always in the same place. In Sheet 1, add a label at the first

	A	B	C	D	E
1	GOOG quote		Real-time quotes		
2	421.18 up+21.72 +5.44%fyi				
3	fyi Volume	12.56 Mil	GOOG Intraday Chart		
4	fyi Avg Daily Volume	10.5 Mil	Intraday Chart		
5	Day's High	423.51	NASDAQ Exchange		
6	Day's Low	405.73	5d 1m 3m 1y 3y 5y 10y		
7	Open	407.38	Data Source: CSI 12:14 PM ET		
8	Previous Close	399.46	Quotes delayed 15 minutes		
9	Bid	421.08			
10	Bid Size	500			
11	Ask	421.18			
12	Ask Size	100	Current Div. Yield	NA	
13	52 Week High	475.11	Market Cap.	124.5 Bil	
14	52 Week Low	172.57	Tot. Shares Out.	295.5 Mil	
15	Instit. Ownership	51.00%	Forward P/E	67.3	
16	P/E	88.2	Sales	5.251 Bil	
17	Earnings/Share	4.53	Return on Equity	14.8	
18	Div/Share	NA	Beta	-0.07	
19					
20					

Figure P3-18   P/E Ratio > 20 (in Worksheet Cell B16)

Figure P3-19   Setting the Conditional Formatting for when the P/E Ratio < 18

blank row at the bottom of Column A—"52 Week Range." In the cell next to your label in column B, enter this formula:

=VLOOKUP("52 Week High", '[Sheet 1]Sheet1'!$A:$B,2,) - VLOOKUP("52 Week Low", '[Sheet 1]Sheet1'!$A:$B,2,)

You will be prompted for your file name and the worksheet, so save it to your worksheet and Sheet 1. You should see your calculated value as shown in Figure P3-21 (with black border).

Example 2: Futures

Start a new worksheet. From the Excel menu, using your mouse, select Data—Import External Data—New Web Query. You should see a window open, as shown in Figure P3-22. In the address box (A), type http://www.cbot.com/cbot/pub/page/0,3181,1544,00.html.

Then click the Go button (B). Scroll down a little to reveal the price table for the 10-year Treasury notes contract, using the scroll bar control on the right (C). For readers new to the scroll bar, you

	A	B	C	D	E
			Microsoft Excel - StockTableExample1		
	CBH quote		Real-time quotes		CBH
1	CBH quote		Real-time quotes		CBH
2	32.35 up+0.14 +0.43%				
3	Volume	569,500	CBH Intraday Chart		
4	Avg Daily Volume	2.178 Mil	Intraday Chart		
5	Day's High	32.57	NYSE Exchange		
6	Day's Low	32.15	5d 1m 3m 1y 3y 5y 10y		
7	fyi Open	32.21	Data Source: CSI 12:50 PM ET		
8	Previous Close	32.21	Quotes delayed 20 minutes		
9	Bid	NA			
10	Bid Size	1,800			
11	Ask	NA			
12	Ask Size	500	Current Div. Yield	1.5	
13	52 Week High	35.98	Market Cap.	5.618 Bil	
14	52 Week Low	26.87	Tot. Shares Out.	173.7 Mil	
15	Instit. Ownership	87.10%	Forward P/E	17.7	
16	fyi P/E	17.9	Sales	1.986 Bil	
17	Earnings/Share	1.8	Return on Equity	14.7	
18	fyi Div/Share	0.48	Beta	0.59	
19					
20					

Figure P3-20   P/E Ratio of 17.9 (<18) in Worksheet Cell B16

can click on the little arrowhead at the bottom or click and drag the blue scroll button in the center of the control. To click and drag, just hold the left mouse button down while the mouse pointer is placed over the scroll button, and then pull the mouse down (toward you). Click on the black arrow in the yellow square next to the table (D). You should see the arrow change to a check mark on a blue square. Then click on the Import button (E).

Then you will see a window that should look like the one shown in Figure P3-2. Click on the OK button (A) and you should see the worksheet fill up with the table values, as shown in Figure P3-23.

	A				
	B19	▼	*fx* =VLOOKUP("52 Week High", '[Sheet 1]Sheet1'!$A:$B,2,) -		
	A		VLOOKUP("52 Week Low", '[Sheet 1]Sheet1'!$A:$B,2,)		
1	GOOG quote		Real-time quotes		
2	421.18 up+21.72 +5.44%fyi				
3	fyi Volume	12.56 Mil	GOOG Intraday Chart		
4	fyi Avg Daily Volume	10.5 Mil	Intraday Chart		
5	Day's High	423.51	NASDAQ Exchange		
6	Day's Low	405.73	5d 1m 3m 1y 3y 5y 10y		
7	Open	407.38	Data Source: CSI 12:14 PM ET		
8	Previous Close	399.46	Quotes delayed 15 minutes		
9	Bid	421.08			
10	Bid Size	500			
11	Ask	421.18			
12	Ask Size	100	Current Div. Yield	NA	
13	52 Week High	475.11	Market Cap.	124.5 Bil	
14	52 Week Low	172.57	Tot. Shares Out.	295.5 Mil	
15	Instit. Ownership	51.00%	Forward P/E	67.3	
16	P/E	88.2	Sales	5.251 Bil	
17	Earnings/Share	4.53	Return on Equity	14.8	
18	Div/Share	NA	Beta	-0.07	
19	52 Week Range	302.54			

Figure P3-21   Calculated Value for the 52-Week Range in Worksheet (Cell B19)

(For a further explanation of this window, see the example for stocks earlier in this chapter.)

Notice how the first column (A) is very wide. To make it narrower, position the mouse pointer over the border between columns A and B at the top, as shown in Figure P3-24 (in the black square). The mouse pointer should change to a vertical bar with a double pointing horizontal arrow, as shown in that figure. Hold down the left mouse button and drag the mouse to the left to resize the column width.

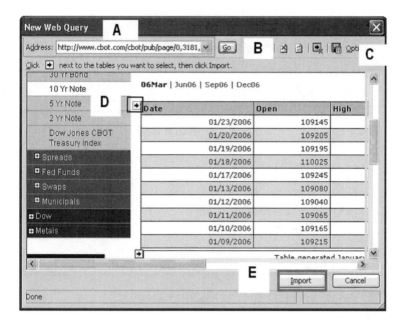

Figure P3-22   Selecting the Table for March 2006 10-Year Note from the New Web Pop-up Dialog

To freeze your column headers so that they will always be visible no matter how far down you scroll in your worksheet, click on cell A2 (for a definition of a cell, see the earlier in this chapter example), as shown in Figure P3-25 (A). Select Window—Freeze panes from the Excel top menu (B). Then create a header for a new column for the daily range by typing "Range" at the top of column F (C).

Now we need to calculate the daily range. Enter this formula into the cell at F2: =c2-d2, as shown in Figure P3-26 (bordered in black) and hit the Enter key.

You should see the value for the first date's daily range, as shown in Figure P3-27 (A).

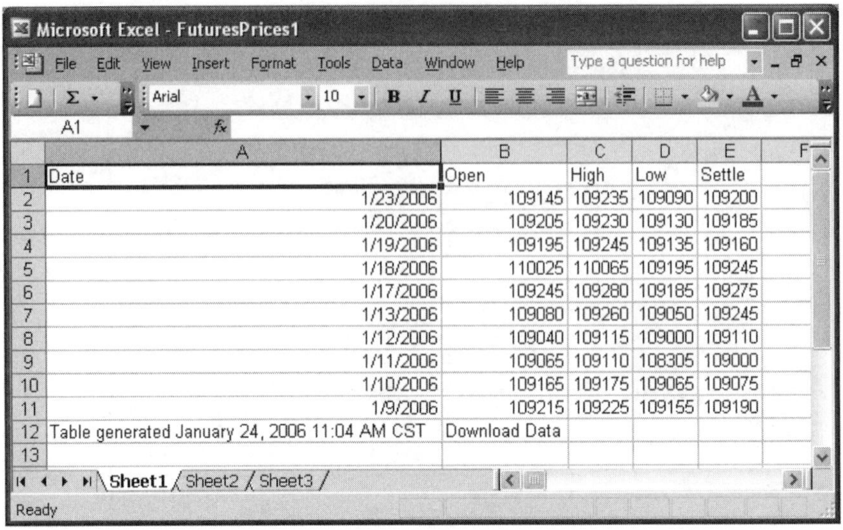

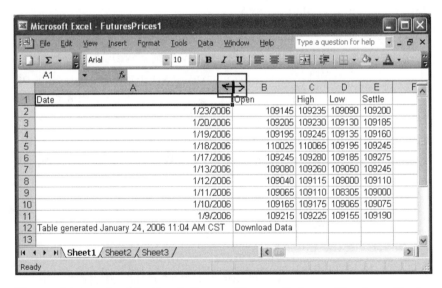

Figure P3-23   Imported Table Data in the Worksheet

Figure P3-24   Double-Head Arrow Mouse Pointer (Used to Resize Column Width in the Worksheet)

Now you need to take a few more steps to fill up the Range column with values. First click in cell F2, as shown in Figure P3-27 (B). Then choose Edit—Copy from the top menu (A). You will see the border of cell F2 become a moving dotted line. Now select the cells to copy the formula into with your mouse by clicking and dragging, as shown in Figure P3-28 (outlined in black and shaded in gray). Hit the Enter key.

You should now see your Range column filled with values, as shown in Figure P3-29.

Now calculate the average daily range. Click on the cell just beneath your column of values for the range and then click on the sum button, as shown in Figure P3-30 (A). You will see your entire column of values with a moving dotted line border around them and a default formula displayed (=SUM(F2:F11), as shown in Figure P3-30. All you need to do now is hit the Enter key.

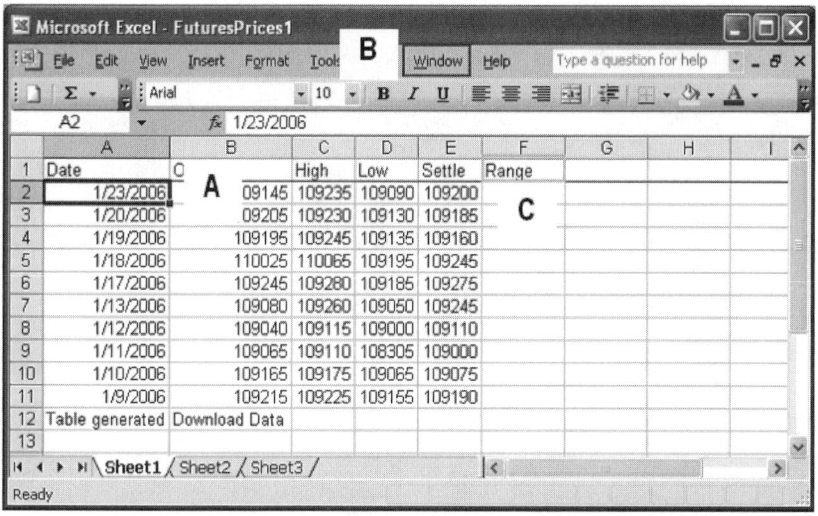

Figure P3-25   Clicking on Cell A2 in the Worksheet Prior to Freezing the Column Headers in the Top Row

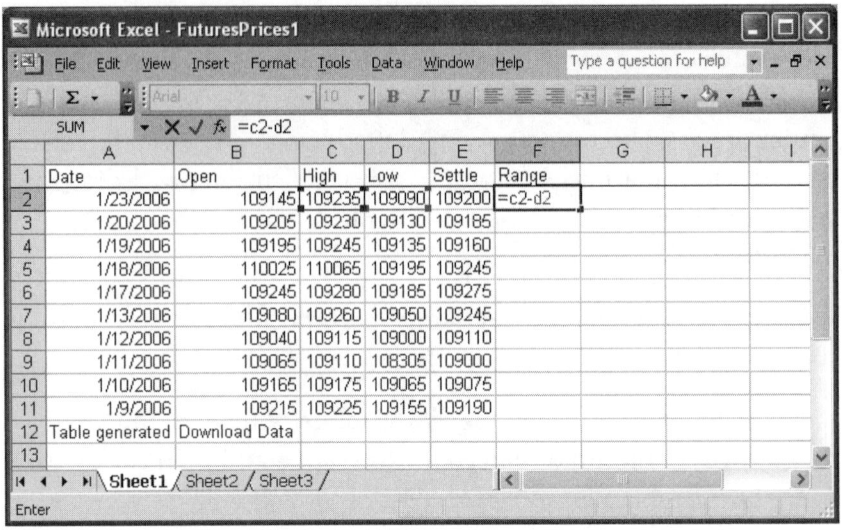

	A	B	C	D	E	F
1	Date	Open	High	Low	Settle	Range
2	1/23/2006	109145	109235	109090	109200	=c2-d2
3	1/20/2006	109205	109230	109130	109185	
4	1/19/2006	109195	109245	109135	109160	
5	1/18/2006	110025	110065	109195	109245	
6	1/17/2006	109245	109280	109185	109275	
7	1/13/2006	109080	109260	109050	109245	
8	1/12/2006	109040	109115	109000	109110	
9	1/11/2006	109065	109110	108305	109000	
10	1/10/2006	109165	109175	109065	109075	
11	1/9/2006	109215	109225	109155	109190	
12	Table generated	Download Data				
13						

Figure P3-26 Entering the Formula to Calculate the Daily Range in Cell F2 of the Worksheet

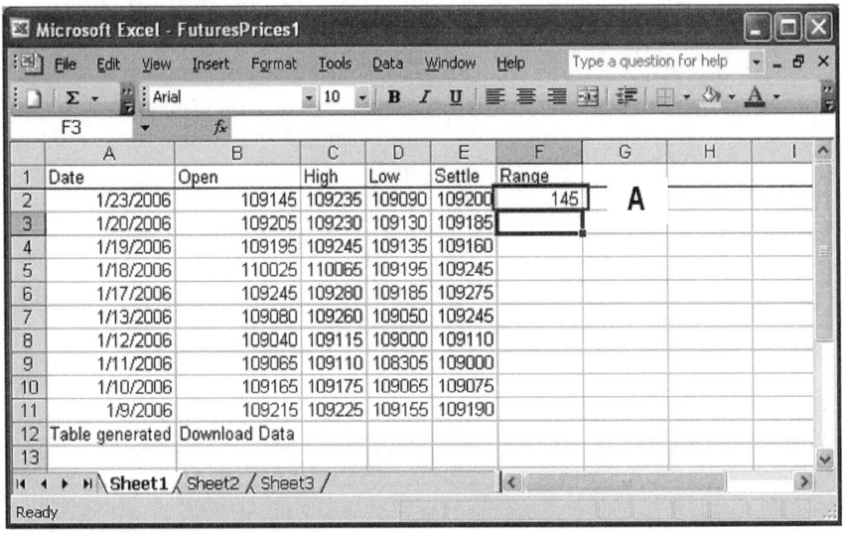

	A	B	C	D	E	F
1	Date	Open	High	Low	Settle	Range
2	1/23/2006	109145	109235	109090	109200	145
3	1/20/2006	109205	109230	109130	109185	
4	1/19/2006	109195	109245	109135	109160	
5	1/18/2006	110025	110065	109195	109245	
6	1/17/2006	109245	109280	109185	109275	
7	1/13/2006	109080	109260	109050	109245	
8	1/12/2006	109040	109115	109000	109110	
9	1/11/2006	109065	109110	108305	109000	
10	1/10/2006	109165	109175	109065	109075	
11	1/9/2006	109215	109225	109155	109190	
12	Table generated	Download Data				
13						

Figure P3-27 The Calculated Daily Range for January 23, 2006 in Cell F2

	A	B	C	D	E	F
1	Date	Open	High	Low	Settle	Range
2	1/23/2006	109145	109235	109090	109200	145
3	1/20/2006	109205	109230	109130	109185	
4	1/19/2006	109195	109245	109135	109160	
5	1/18/2006	110025	110065	109195	109245	
6	1/17/2006	109245	109280	109185	109275	
7	1/13/2006	109080	109260	109050	109245	
8	1/12/2006	109040	109115	109000	109110	
9	1/11/2006	109065	109110	108305	109000	
10	1/10/2006	109165	109175	109065	109075	
11	1/9/2006	109215	109225	109155	109190	
12	Table generated	Download Data				
13						

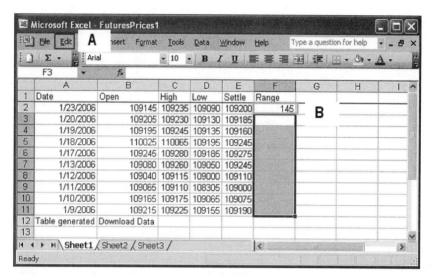

Figure P3-28 Selecting the Cells into Which the Daily Range Calculation Formula Is to Be Copied

	A	B	C	D	E	F
1	Date	Open	High	Low	Settle	Range
2	1/23/2006	109145	109235	109090	109200	145
3	1/20/2006	109205	109230	109130	109185	100
4	1/19/2006	109195	109245	109135	109160	110
5	1/18/2006	110025	110065	109195	109245	870
6	1/17/2006	109245	109280	109185	109275	95
7	1/13/2006	109080	109260	109050	109245	210
8	1/12/2006	109040	109115	109000	109110	115
9	1/11/2006	109065	109110	108305	109000	805
10	1/10/2006	109165	109175	109065	109075	110
11	1/9/2006	109215	109225	109155	109190	70
12	Table generated	Download Data				
13						

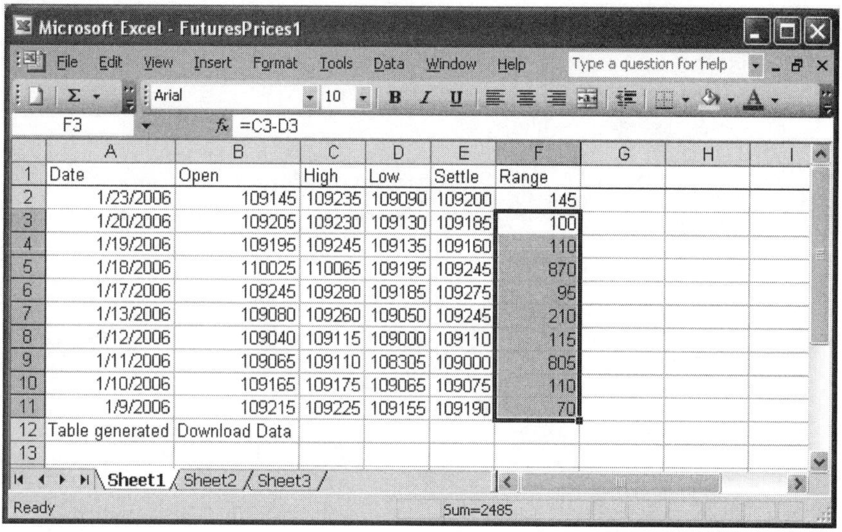

Figure P3-29 The Calculated Daily Ranges in Column F

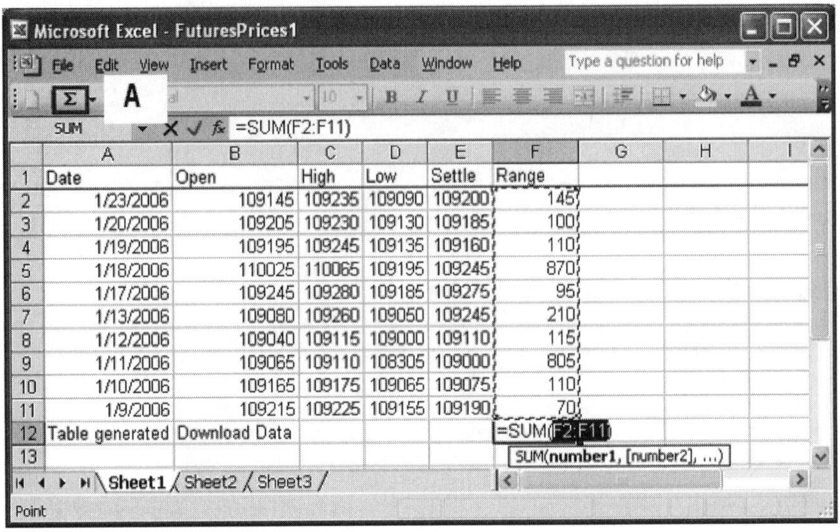

	A	B	C	D	E	F
1	Date	Open	High	Low	Settle	Range
2	1/23/2006	109145	109235	109090	109200	145
3	1/20/2006	109205	109230	109130	109185	100
4	1/19/2006	109195	109245	109135	109160	110
5	1/18/2006	110025	110065	109195	109245	870
6	1/17/2006	109245	109280	109185	109275	95
7	1/13/2006	109080	109260	109050	109245	210
8	1/12/2006	109040	109115	109000	109110	115
9	1/11/2006	109065	109110	108305	109000	805
10	1/10/2006	109165	109175	109065	109075	110
11	1/9/2006	109215	109225	109155	109190	70
12	Table generated	Download Data				=SUM(F2:F11)
13						

Figure P3-30 Entering the Formula to Calculate the Sum of All the Daily Range for the Period in Cell F12

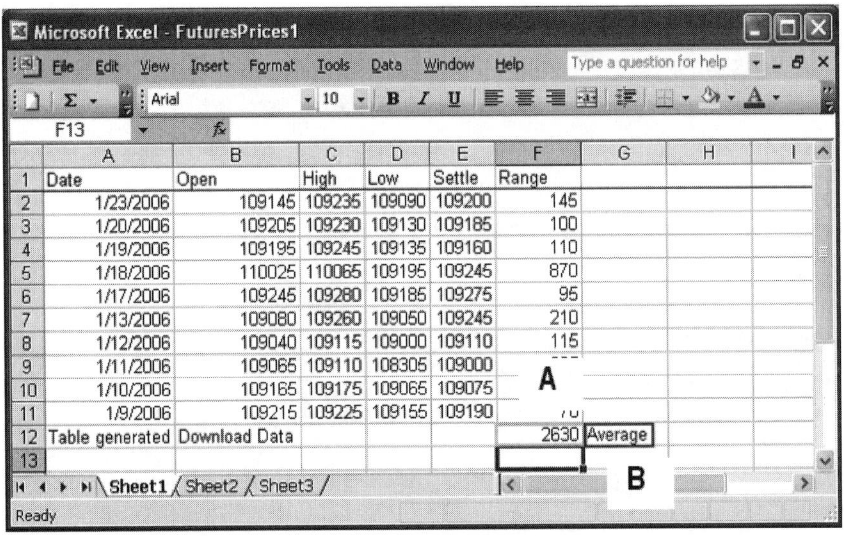

	A	B	C	D	E	F	G
1	Date	Open	High	Low	Settle	Range	
2	1/23/2006	109145	109235	109090	109200	145	
3	1/20/2006	109205	109230	109130	109185	100	
4	1/19/2006	109195	109245	109135	109160	110	
5	1/18/2006	110025	110065	109195	109245	870	
6	1/17/2006	109245	109280	109185	109275	95	
7	1/13/2006	109080	109260	109050	109245	210	
8	1/12/2006	109040	109115	109000	109110	115	
9	1/11/2006	109065	109110	108305	109000		
10	1/10/2006	109165	109175	109065	109075		
11	1/9/2006	109215	109225	109155	109190		
12	Table generated	Download Data				2630	Average
13							

Figure P3-31 Typing the Label for the Average Daily Range in Cell G12

You should see the sum of all the daily ranges, as shown in Figure P3-31 (A).

Add a text label next to your value by clicking to the cell to the right and typing "Average" (B).

Obtaining the average daily range is simply a matter of modifying the formula in the cell where you calculated the sum of the daily ranges to divide that value by 10. Click on that cell. Then, at the end of the formula in the edit box above it, as shown in Figure P3-32 (A), add/10 to the end of the formula, and hit the Enter key. You should see your calculated average of the daily range, as shown in Figure P3-32 (B).

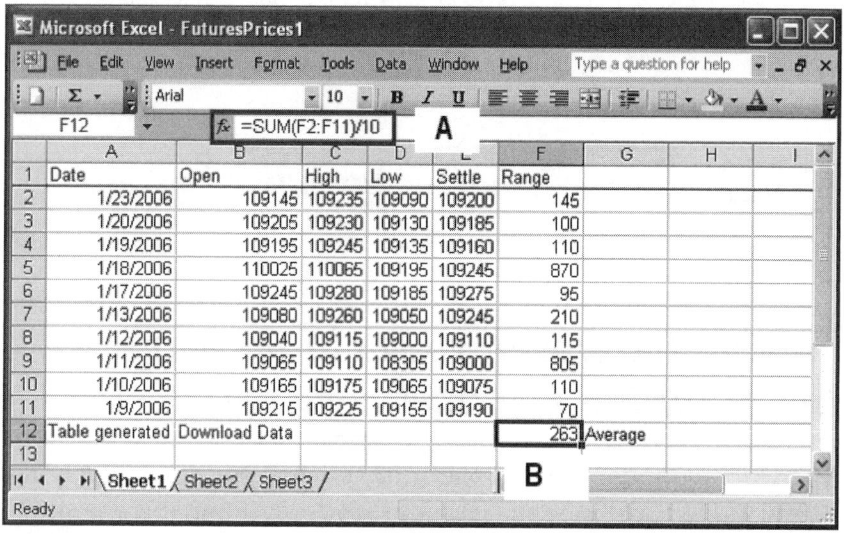

	A	B	C	D	E	F	G
1	Date	Open	High	Low	Settle	Range	
2	1/23/2006	109145	109235	109090	109200	145	
3	1/20/2006	109205	109230	109130	109185	100	
4	1/19/2006	109195	109245	109135	109160	110	
5	1/18/2006	110025	110065	109195	109245	870	
6	1/17/2006	109245	109280	109185	109275	95	
7	1/13/2006	109080	109260	109050	109245	210	
8	1/12/2006	109040	109115	109000	109110	115	
9	1/11/2006	109065	109110	108305	109000	805	
10	1/10/2006	109165	109175	109065	109075	110	
11	1/9/2006	109215	109225	109155	109190	70	
12	Table generated	Download Data				263	Average

Figure P3-32 Modifying the Formula in Cell F12 to Obtain the Average Daily Range for the Period

Trader's Notebook 2

Understanding the Odds

By Bob Hunt

*Bob Hunt, creator of the Pattern Trapper online trading course
and editor of the Pattern Trapper Futures Trading Newsletter,
has long been involved in developing charting platform software
add-ons to help beginning and experienced traders hone their
discretionary trading skills. For more information, contact Bob at
Rhunt@ PatternTrapper.com or on the Web at www.Pattern
Trapper.com.*

Minimum Activity									Maximum Activity
	0	1	2	3	4	5	6	7	8

Trading the Opening Gap in the Mini Index Futures Contract

Many active traders regard the futures markets as unsuitable for them largely because of the assumption that the endeavor requires massive amounts of time and energy. Effective *full-time* trading does require a serious commitment, but an initial introduction does not require that the participant be chained to a computer screen all day. Effective trading *can*, and for many successful traders *does*, consist of employing only one or two high-probability setups that regularly occur during specific periods of the day. These traders have done their research, fully understand the odds behind their methodology, and execute their trades in a very disciplined fashion. The purpose of this chapter is to explore one high-probability setup that normally occurs within a single specific period of the trading day: the opening gap.

An opening gap occurs when the market begins the trading day at a price different from the one at which it closed at the end of the previous session, resulting in a "gap" in price when viewed on an intraday chart. If this discrepancy is unusually large, it is likely that new information has entered the marketplace, and price activity will tend to trend even further in the gap direction. If the difference between the closing and opening price levels falls within a more reasonable range, there will be a tendency for the market to trade back into the gap area. The strength of this tendency is indirectly proportional to the magnitude of the gap. The narrower the gap, the stronger the tendency. Very small gaps are not even tradable. Very large gaps are less likely to close and contain the potential to move quickly even farther from the gap level, marking the beginning of a strong trend move. These kinds of gaps are referred to as a *breakaway*. In contrast, the kinds of gaps that have a higher probability of closure and the sort we are most interested in for the purposes of this chapter are referred to as *Common* gaps (see Figures P3-33 and P3-34).

There are no hard-and-fast rules that make one gap a breakaway and another common, but a few general guidelines can be used to differentiate between the two. The first is time-based. If the opening price on a gap to the upside stands as the low after the first 30 minutes of trading, the gap most likely is of the breakaway kind. On a downside gap, if the opening price remains the highest price traded within the first 30 minutes, there is a high likelihood that the gap is of a breakaway nature. Another consideration is the magnitude of the gap. An opening gap level that falls below the levels noted in Table P3-1 *generally* can be regarded as common. Gap

Figure P3-33   Breakaway Gap

Figure P3-34   Common Gap

levels that are greater than the ones noted in the table can be thought of as breakaway. If a gap level falls between the two, one can think of it as having an equal chance of developing as common or breakaway. Remember that these levels are to be used only as a very rough rule of thumb. They are relevant at the time of publication but may vary to some degree with changing market conditions.

Table P3-1   Gap Size Guidelines

Market	Common	Breakaway
S&P 500 E-Mini (ES)	<4.00 points	>7.00 points
Dow Jones Mini (YM)	<40 points	>70 points
Nasdaq 100 E-Mini (NQ)	<10.00 points	>18.00 points
Russell 2000 E-Mini (ER)	<2.00 points	>3.50 points

A third method used to differentiate between the two is based on NYSE tick readings. The tick is provided by most intraday data providers and at any given moment represents the number of stocks trading higher on the NYSE minus the number of stocks trading lower. A positive reading is bullish, as it indicates a greater number of issues increasing in price, whereas a negative reading is bearish. An opening gap to the upside that cannot exceed a NYSE tick reading of +300 within the first few minutes of trading generally is considered to be of a common nature. In contrast, an upside gap that occurs on a tick reading greater than +300 and climbs as the price climbs usually is regarded as breakaway. Alternatively, a downside gap that does not drop below −300 within the first few minutes can be considered common, whereas one that occurs on a tick reading that drops below −300 and drops as the price drops can be considered breakaway. Again, it must be emphasized that these parameters are best regarded as a rough rule of thumb and should not be used in a mechanical fashion. Think of them as extra bits of information that assist you in interpreting internal market dynamics.

In addition to the guidelines mentioned above, there are a few market variables that one should take into account before the start of the trading day. These considerations aid a trader in determining the likely nature of trading activity in the early hours and help the trader decide whether the opening gap (if one exists) is likely to be tradable. First off is a review of the trin, which sometimes is called the Arms Index in honor of its developer, Richard Arms. This is a breadth oscillator that is designed to measure internal market strength and most often is provided as part of a real-time data feed. Although a modified version of trin is preferred because it delivers more detailed information and is far easier to read (this is especially important during fast-paced, hectic trading conditions), the levels noted here reflect the standard trin, which is more easily accessible for most readers. A closing prior day trin reading near or above 2.0 indicates that the day ended on an excessively bearish note. If overnight pricing has not swung to the upside, one usually can expect it to do so in the very early part of the trading day. Once this excessive bearish pressure is released, further downside pressure typically follows. In contrast, if the prior day trin finished near or lower than 0.5, traders know that the day ended with excessive bullishness. A push lower should occur either in overnight trading or early the next day. Once the market tone is effectively neutralized, a further upside normally ensues.

Just before the market opens it is also a good idea to mark on an intraday chart the price high and low points that occurred in overnight trading (all trading activity that occurred since the prior day close). If market activity is thought of as an auction process in which bidders and sellers constantly vie for the most advantageous price, overnight highs and lows represent the outer extremes of accepted value for that particular period. The highest price achieved represents the maximum that buyers were willing to offer, and the lowest price represents the minimum that sellers were willing to accept. For this reason, subsequent price action has a tendency to remain within the boundaries of apparent value as defined during this period. If these limits are exceeded on the upside, traders know that current market activity has a bullish tone. In contrast, any downside push that surpasses the overnight low has bearish implications.

As the market nears its opening bell and the actual gap size is better known, traders concentrate on a set of statistics that describe the odds of price returning to the prior day's closing level. If one uses gap level historical price information, the market-specific probability of closure can be calculated and displayed as a known value just before the beginning of each trading day (see Figure P3-35). This information is dependent on the direction and size of the gap and can indicate what the chances for full closure happen to be along with the

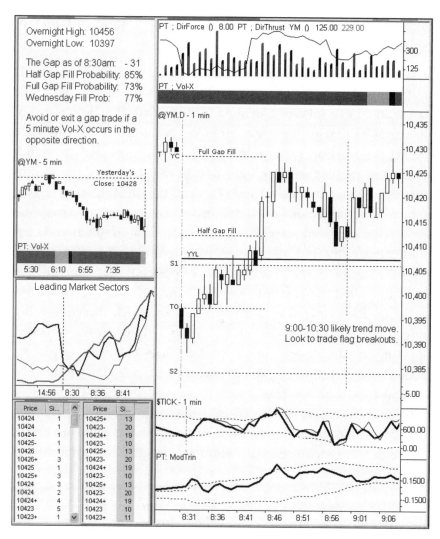

Figure P3-35   An Opening Gap Trading Opportunity

odds of half-gap closure (which are always greater than those of full closure). One also can determine the probability of closure based on the current day of the week as well as note any other significant variables that may affect the probability of gap closure, such as special precautions necessary on the day after options expiration Friday or on "first Friday" employment report days.

With this information in hand and assuming that the gap size is tradable with a high probability of closure, a trader can begin the day with an eye toward placing a trade in that direction. Some of the variables that are best monitored just before placing a gap trade are (1) price action relative to significant support and resistance levels (i.e., regular session highs and lows established on each of the prior two trading days) and (2) NYSE tick readings as a sign of a short-term trend exhaustion. It is especially important to measure the market's current state of expansion and/or contraction. Is the market currently trading in an ever-tightening range, or has it just begun a strong move in a direction opposite to gap closure? An indicator called the volatility expansion meter, referred to as Vol-X in Figure P3-35, can indicate when and in which direction a big move is likely to begin. If Vol-X is firing a signal in the direction opposite to gap closure, one definitely does *not* want to place a trade in the direction of gap closure. Instead, a trader wants to be looking for a trade in the same direction as the gap. Although a detailed explanation of Vol-X is outside the scope of this chapter, the standard application of Bollinger Bands can provide a similar, although less precise, glimpse into these kinds of internal market dynamics.

As an example, refer to Figure P3-35, which depicts an opening gap trading opportunity in the Dow Jones mini contract. The indicator in the top left screen reports gap size, direction, and accompanying statistics before and at the moment the market opens (all time references are basis the Central Time Zone). This indicator suggests that the odds for closure are high and that a trader wants to look for an early opportunity to get long. The "Leading Market Sectors" chart directly below the gap statistics display indicates that the three sectors that often lead market activity are starting the day with a definite bullish bias, adding another reason to be on the long side. In the large one-minute candlestick chart one can see that Vol-X has not fired a signal to the short side, and this indicates that range expansion lower is unlikely. Perhaps the most significant factor affecting the decision to take this trade is that the NYSE tick reading ($TICK) is unable to muster any momentum to the downside. In fact, it cannot even break down through the zero level. The rise in tick readings is the trigger into the trade, which gets the trader in a few points before the 10397 level of today's open is breached. A protective stop is placed just below the closest known support zone, which is S2 at 10384.

The market moves in the trader's favor in rapid fashion, finding only temporary resistance along S1 and YYL (the daily low two days before today's trading). The half gap fill line is surpassed quickly as the market moves on to reach the full gap fill target of 10428. The trade nets a total of 33 points, or $165 per contract minus commission and fees. It is also worth pointing out that the market made a short-term bounce away from this level once the gap was filled. This is a common occurrence. A stop and reverse placed at the gap fill level often can garner a few extra points of profit. Again, NYSE tick readings can confirm the reversal point as well as serve as the exit trigger.

In summary, successful gap trading requires a series of considerations taken (1) before the market opens, (2) as the market opens, and (3) 30 minutes after the market opens if the gap has not yet closed:

1. Before the market opens:

   - Prior day closing trin readings: A closing trin near or above 2.0 typically results in an early swing to the upside. A trin near or lower than 0.5 can mean a swing to the downside.

- Mark overnight highs and lows that may act as potential support or resistance within the gap area.

2. As the market opens:

- Use Table P3-1 to determine its common or breakaway status on the basis of the magnitude of the gap.

- Assess the probability of closure on the basis of gap level historical price information derived from your own statistical research or from software designed to perform this task.

- Pay attention to opening NYSE tick readings. An upside gap on tick readings less than $+300$ is likely to close, as is a downside gap on Tick readings greater than -300 (i.e., -100).

3. Thirty minutes after the market opens:

- If the open on an upside gap is the lowest price traded during the first 30 minutes, the gap is probably breakaway, as would be a downside gap whose open is the high of the first 30 minutes. Look for opportunities to participate in the direction of the gap rather than against it.

To paraphrase a song made popular by Kenny Rogers in the late 1970s, a successful trader "knows when to hold 'em and knows when to fold 'em." For those traders, effective trading has become a constant process of creating action plans in direct response to consistently changing market conditions. They participate only if the market develops according to their plan. If it does not, they simply fold 'em and walk away with their eye on the next potential setup. The opening gap trade in the index offers one high-potential action plan. Learn to trade it effectively and you'll be a significant step closer to long-term, consistent success.

Trader's
Notebook 3

The Rohr Report

Minimum  Maximum
Activity   0   1   2   3   4   5   6   7   8   Activity

Courtesy of my friend Alan Rohrbach at Rohr International, Inc., I was able to get this brief piece of in-depth, longer-term analysis that institutional dealers can afford to pay for and utilize. Rohrbach publishes insightful major trend background, along with thorough, highly regarded technical projections. Below is an interesting insight into the Federal Reserve's agenda in 2006. This is a very limited sample of Rohr's extensive analysis of various political and economic influences.

As one would expect, institutional analysis is expensive. At the time of this writing, Rohr charges $6,000 per year just for the daily technical and background letter, and direct consultation can cost tens of thousands of dollars per year. That is what it takes to benefit from insights developed over decades of successful trend research. However, as a way to give back to the industry, Rohr International also is involved in education, training, and mentoring programs. (Alan can be reached at AR.Rohr.Intl@Comcast.net.)

Capital Markets Observer
Volume II Number 3: Wednesday, January 18, 2006

Reports and Events, Markets, the Fed, US Dollar, Energy Insecurity

The Fed

While there are quite a few folks who believe a weak outlook in today's Beige Book will bring any further rate hikes from the Fed to a precipitous end, we beg to differ. Our reasons for this go back to that same psychology that was in place since the FOMC did not use the potential weakness from Hurricane Katrina's impact to pause, and remains as follows (with the previously stated caveat that signs of a bona fide recession beginning this quarter could change the outlook for Mr. Bernanke's decision at his first meeting on March 28):

REPRINTED FROM *CMO* I-10 (Thursday, November 2, 2005)
MR. GREENSPAN
The retention of "removal of accommodation" language yesterday is a clear sign that (barring any precipitous decline in the equity markets) the Fed is on a glide path toward a 4.75% Federal Funds rate by the end of Mr. Bernanke's first meeting as Chairman at the end of March. If you feel that's an audacious assumption, consider these five related points:

1. At 4.00% the current Federal Funds rate is still accommodative by historic standards that imply it has not become restrictive until it is at least one-half to one full percentage point above projected GDP growth;
2. The Fed wants rates as high as possible prior to Mr. Greenspan's retirement so that his successor does not need to raise rates in a way that brings disdain upon the Fed for causing a recession (which is exactly the situation that Mr. Greenspan was stuck with when Mr. Volcker handed over the reins);

3. In any event, the Fed will not be signaling that it has put through the *penultimate* rate hike until it eliminates the "removal of accommodation" language. On current form that means the earliest they might hold steady will be Mr. Greenspan's last meeting as Chairman in January;

4. Yet, to hold steady in January would create an expectation that they had finished the tightening cycle, and leave quite a bit of pressure on Mr. Bernanke to make his first move as Chairman an easing;

5. Which is an untenable position for a new Chairman, as regardless of anything else (short of an obvious recession beginning in February or early March) Mr. Bernanke's first task as Chairman is to establish his anti-inflation credentials, and worry about the full employment portion of the Fed's mandate only once that is addressed.

—Rohr

Trader's Notebook 4

Trading Software Companies

Minimum Activity   0 1 2 3 4 5 6 7 8   Maximum Activity

Trading Software Company: TradePortal

Company Web site: www.tradeportal.com

SUMMARY   TradePortal.com, Inc., provides trading software to hedge funds, market makers, and active traders. MatrixSuite is a group of trading applications used by institutions and real-time back office administrative tools for easy management. MatrixSuite consists of TradeMatrix for the retail market, ProMatrix for hedge funds, and MarketMatrix for market makers. TradePortal also has a very useful educational section on its Web site that can help active traders.

TRADEMATRIX   TradeMatrix is a trading software application that is used by all levels of active traders. It provides access to market data, executions, profits and losses, and so forth. Simulator and demo accounts are available for free. TradePortal offers computer technical support at an 800 number and by e-mail. Refer to the company Web site for additional information.

The following material contains excerpts from the www.tradeportal.com Web site.

For Active Traders

SELECTED SOFTWARE FEATURES

Integrated Trading Tabs
  Trade all liquidity instruments from one trading window.
  Trade Nasdaq, over-the-counter securities.
  Trade New York Stock Exchange listed securities.
  Trade Options on all the available exchanges.

Hot Keys   Advanced order entry through keyboard stroke combinations; fully customizable and easy-to-use interface.

Rapid Point and Click Order Entry   Mouse-driven order entry through click entries into the level II montage. Click to buy, sell, or short a security.

Order Defaults   Order default Settings for a single (local) trading window. Shares (adjustable to open position), route, order type, time in force, display quantity, random reserver, discretion, peg type, peg offset, and account

Stop Order   Use to send an order to sell a stock when its price falls to a particular point, thus limiting the loss.

Trend Indicator   Records the last eight ticks and displays the information in a graphical color band that gauges the near-term tick trend.

Advanced Order Management System   Set order entry conditions around a specific symbol. The intelligent symbol orders are based on premarket, market, and postmarket trading.

Flexible Portfolio Management   View account status with order messages, orders, fills, trades, or positions or by average price.

Minimal Computer Configuration

- Windows: XP Home or XP Professional.
- Processor: 2.5-GHz processor or faster.
- Random-access memory: at least 256 MB.
- Hard drive: 100 gigabytes.
- 19-inch monitor: 1024 × 728 16-bit color.
- Windows browser: Internet Explorer 6 or Mozilla Firefox 1.0 or higher.
- Recommended connection: T1, cable modem, or DSL. Do not use dial-up.

All copyrights and trademarks are the property of their respective owners.

Trading Software Company: eFloorTrade, LLC

Company Web site: www.efloortrade.com

Summary

eFloorTrade (EFT) provides trading software for a variety of solutions in trading futures. EFT algorithmic trading strategies are incorporated into the eFloorTrader software platform. These algorithmic strategies permit the trader to identify opportunities in the markets immediately.

Brokerage Services

Active traders can use the EFT software for multiple accounts and use it simultaneously with multiple clearing firms. EFT offers clearing through these multiple trading platforms. The EFT platform provides an audit trail of orders placed, featuring time stamping and storage of electronic records to meet regulatory requirements. The eFloorTrade commission rates are derived from monthly volume.

EFT offers simulator and demo accounts at its Web site for free, and computer technical support is available at an 800 number and by e-mail. Refer to the company Web site for additional information.

The following material contains excerpts from the www. efloortrade.com Web site.

For Active Traders

SELECTED SOFTWARE FEATURES

eFloor Trade News   Government reports, trading news articles, and numerous exchanges such as the CBOT, CME, and CBOE. EFT also provides active traders with numerous online seminars and scheduled related events.

Professional Services
- Universal autoexecution trading platform
- Back-up platform for trade executions
- Downloadable and exportable trade activity
- Sophisticated trading tools and technology
- Block trading or easy segregation of accounts
- Commitment to improving and developing new technology

Proprietary Trading Firm Services   EFT is an independent introducing broker to firms that use EFT electronic trading tools. The programs and execution platform are available through Man Financial, Cargill, Rosenthal Collins, Alaron Futures, O'Connor, and GNI London.

Retail Services   EFT assigns an account executive to each account, from discount to full-service.

Trading Simulator Platforms   EFT offers J-Trader, X-Trader, eFloorTrader, and MTrade real-time simulators. The eFloorTrade simulator data uses fills based on real order flow. This feature permits the testing of trading strategies in real time before a trader risks real capital. The EFT simulator permits scalping of multiple electronic markets simultaneously and has an autoexecution functionality.

Futures Options Trading Features
   Long calls/puts
   Short calls/puts
   spreads
   Combos
   Covered calls
   Straddles
   Butterflies
   Condors
   Collars ratio
   Spreads

Minimal Computer Configuration
   • Windows: XP Home or XP Professional
   • Processor: 2.5-GHz processor or faster
   • Random-access memory: at least 256 MB
   • Hard drive: 100 gigabytes
   • 19-inch Monitor: 1024 × 728 16 bit color

- Windows browser: Internet Explorer 6 or Mozilla Firefox 1.0 or higher
- Recommended connection: T1, cable modem, or DSL. Do not use dial-up.

All copyrights and trademarks are the property of their respective owners.

Trading Software Company: eSignal, an Interactive Data Corporation

Company Web site: www.esignal.com

SUMMARY   eSignal provides a robust trading software solution that features real-time market data and information for active traders. eSignal has over 20 years of experience in providing financial information such as global real-time market data to active traders, investors, and financial professionals worldwide. The company offers eSignal as its main product, with real-time quote services to provide continuous time-sensitive financial data via the Internet to computers or workstations connected over the Internet.

eSignal provides software applications and services such as market quotes for stocks, options, charts, futures, research, news alerts, and back testing. eSignal also offers 'MarketCenter LIVE', a real-time browser-based market quotation service for real-time data on stocks, futures, and options quotes. MarketCenter LIVE includes news, commentary, historical charts, and market statistics.

eSignal offers a robust trading software platform used by all levels of active traders. It features access to extensive market data on futures and options from numerous exchanges. Simulator and demo accounts are available for free. eSignal offers computer technical support at an 800 number and by e-mail. eSignal offers a wide variety of free seminars and events so that active traders can learn more about trading. Refer to the company Web site for additional information.

The following material contains excerpts from the www. esignal.com Web site.

FOR ACTIVE TRADERS

Selected Software Features
   Advanced charting
   Data analysis
   Back testing and strategy analyzer
   Charting—standard (basic)
   CME E-Minis CBOT mini-sized futures data
   Equities, options, futures data
   Excel spreadsheet: real-time analysis
   Market in-depth reports: CME, CBOT, Nasdaq, NYSE, Pink
      Sheets, ECNs, Forex
   News and commentary on stocks, futures, and options
   Trade-related world news
   Tick charts, tick bars, seconds bars, and tick volume bars
   Ticker window
   Quote window
   World indexes

Minimal Computer Configuration
   • Windows: XP Home or XP Professional.
   • Processor: 2.5-GHz processor or faster.
   • Random-access memory: at least 256 MB.
   • Hard drive: 100 gigabytes.
   • 19-inch monitor: 1024 × 728 16-bit color.

- Windows browser: Internet Explorer 6 or Mozilla Firefox 1.0 or higher.
- Recommended connection: T1, cable modem, or DSL. Do not use dial-up.

All copyrights and trademarks are the property of their respective owners.

Trading Software Company: TradeStation Securities, Inc.

Company Web site: www.tradestation.com

SUMMARY TradeStation provides a well-established trading software solution that features deep-discount commissions for active traders working in futures, equities, options, and Forex. TradeStation is used by active traders, hedge fund managers, institutions, and exchange members to place strategically executed trades and features a method for automating real-time trades and a method for back testing a trading strategy. TradeStation uses its proprietary EasyLanguage technology to create various scenarios for trading strategies and also executes the trades. EasyLanguage permits back testing of the trading strategy against up to 20 years of actual market data. This feature is useful in reducing the amount of risk incurred during actual real-time trading. However, using TradeStation requires a big commitment of time and energy.

TradeStation can monitor the markets and compare market data with a trader's strategy to identify when to execute the trade, generating entry and exit orders for execution in the marketplace. TradeStation offers simulator and demo accounts for free. Computer technical support is available at an 800 number and by e-mail. TradeStation offers a wide variety of free seminars and tutorials for the active trader to learn more about trading. Refer to the company Web site for additional information. The following material contains excerpts from the www.tradestation.com Web site.

FOR ACTIVE TRADERS

Selected Software Features
- Four-to-one intraday buying power for equities and low overnight and day-trading margin requirements for futures.
- Conflict-free agency-only brokerage services for equities, options, and futures trading.
- Maximum leverage and intraday buying power is calculated and reflected on a real-time basis.

Account Offerings
Individual
IRA
Trust
LLC
Corporate
Sole proprietorship

Minimal Computer Configuration
- Windows: XP Home or XP Professional.
- Processor: 2.5-GHz processor or faster.
- Random-access memory: at least 256 MB.
- Hard drive: 100 gigabytes.
- 19-inch monitor: 1024 × 728 16-bit color.
- Windows browser: Internet Explorer 6 or Mozilla Firefox 1.0 or higher.
- Recommended connection: T1, cable modem, or DSL. Do not use dial-up.

All copyrights and trademarks are the property of their respective owners.

Trading Software Company: Cybertrader— Charles Schwab Corporation

Company Web site: www.cybertrader.com

SUMMARY CyberTrader offers a customizable trading software platform for active traders working with futures, equities, options, and derivatives. Active traders can use the CyberTrader Elite service that features 5,000 trades or 5,000,000 shares per month. Financial services from CyberTrader are used by hedge funds, pension funds, banks, broker-dealers, and portfolio mangers.

A unique feature of CyberTrader is the customizable charts function known as CyberCharts. CyberCharts provide an efficient method for analyzing price and volume movements by using constantly changing market conditions. For instance, futures traders use the charts to analyze E-mini data with 24-hour futures-charting capabilities.

Selected Software Features

Customizable Charts With CyberTrade, traders can customize their charts as they see fit.

Candlestick Charts and Graph Styles Four graph types include point and figure and candlestick and a choice of fonts, colors, and different chart sizes.

Tick Charts, Chart Types, and Overlays Five chart formats are available, including intraday and monthly.

Trend, Support, and Resistance Charts also includes Fibonacci and regression.

Bar Charts and Studies   Technical studies include over 25 types, such as Bollinger Bands, relative strength Index, and stochastics.

CyberTrader offers simulator and demo accounts for free. Computer technical support is available at an 800 number and by e-mail. CyberTrader offers a wide variety of free seminars and tutorials so that active trader can learn more about trading. Refer to the company Web site for additional information.

The following material contains excerpts from the www.cyber-trader.com Web site.

For Active Traders

SELECTED SOFTWARE FEATURES

CyberTrader Simulator   Practice trading 24 hours a day, 7 days a week on the CyberTrader Pro platform with market data.

Online Courses   Learn how to use the trading platform efficiently.

Check InPlay   CyberTrader clients get Briefing.com premium content for free. Daily updates are available on earnings and company and market news.

Ken Tower's Research   Provides daily and weekly market commentary from a chief market strategist.

"Fly on the Wall" Content   Provides recommendations from leading brokerage and investment firms.

Interactive Charting   Features real-time Web-based market charting with statistics and streaming quotes.

Online Newsletter   Provides product analysis, industry news, technical tips, and trader advice.

Minimal Computer Configuration
- Windows: XP Home or XP Professional.
- Processor: 2.5-GHz processor or faster.
- Random-access memory: at least 256 MB.
- Hard drive: 100 gigabytes.
- 19-inch monitor: 1024 × 728 16-bit color
- Windows browser: Internet Explorer 6 or Mozilla Firefox 1.0 or higher.
- Recommended connection: T1, cable modem, or DSL. Do not use dial-up.

All copyrights and trademarks are the property of their respective owners.

Trading Software Company: Qcharts—Lycos Inc.

Company Web site: www.qcharts.com

SUMMARY QCharts offers software trading platforms for active traders, broker-dealers, institutions, and developers. QCharts offers the following three software platforms: QCharts, QCharts Plus, and MetaStock Pro. All three use MB Trading at www. qcharts.mbtrader.com for placing trades of stocks, Dow minis, eMinis, and options. Traders must have or open an account with MB Trading to execute trade orders.

QCharts offers simulator and demo accounts for 30 days for free. Computer technical support is available at an 800 number and by e-mail. QCharts is compatible with a variety of third-party vendors that provide useful fee-based services for active traders. Refer to the company Web site for additional information.

The following material contains excerpts from the www. qcharts.com Web site.

For Active Traders

SELECTED SOFTWARE FEATURES

QCharts Features
- Unlimited symbols and charts
- Nasdaq level II
- Hot list stock scanners
- Customizable quote sheets
- Technical analysis and chart tools
- Historical chart data
- Direct-access trading

QCharts Plus Features
- Option-monitoring tools and montage
- Market downloads
- News, research, and option analysis
- Back testing
- Expert advisories
- Indicator builder
- Advanced charting methods such as equivolume, point and figure, Kagi, Renko, and three line break

Charting Tools
- Bollinger Bands
- Donchian channels
- Moving averages
- Volume at price
- MACD
- Momentum
- RSI
- Stochastics
- Fibonacci time interval
- Andrews pitchfork

Minimal Computer Configuration
- Windows: XP Home or XP Professional.
- Processor: 2.5-GHz processor or faster.
- Random-access memory: at least 256 MB.
- Hard drive: 100 gigabytes.
- 19-inch monitor: 1024 × 728 16-bit color
- Windows browser: Internet Explorer 6 or Mozilla Firefox 1.0 or higher.
- Recommended connection: T1, cable modem, or DSL. Do not use dial-up.

All copyrights and trademarks are the property of their respective owners.

Online Broker: Charles Schwab & Co., Inc.

Company Web site: www.schwab.com

SUMMARY   The Schwab Web site offers a wide variety of financial investment products such as stocks, bonds, and mutual funds. However, its active trader services are equally sophisticated and useful. Schwab's Streetsmart.com simulator for active traders features a simulated real-time trading environment that operates in a 24/7/365 scenario. It is ideal for an active trader who wants to practice trading strategy and execution without opening an account or risking capital.

Schwab simulator accounts are available for a 30-day free trial period. Computer technical support is available at an 800 number and by e-mail. Schwab offers a variety of useful online seminars and in-person workshops to help active traders develop trading skills. Users can upgrade to Streetsmart.com Pro for active trading. Refer to the company Web site for additional information.

The following material contains excerpts from the www. schwab.com Web site.

For Active Traders

SELECTED SOFTWARE FEATURES

Streetsmart.com
- Simulate real-time streaming quotes, news, and charts to keep track of crucial market data.
- Identify price trends by using interactive streaming charts to discover breakouts, reversals, and other time-sensitive trends.
- Display account balances, positions, and transaction information on an updated basis.
- Display conditional orders, trailing stops, streaming real-time quotes, and news.

StreetSmart Pro
- Uses the CyberTrader software engine to display streaming market data on one customizable screen.
- Features conditional alerts and triggers, real-time streaming quotes and news, customized screeners, sector tools, and Nasdaq level II.
- Options trading offers options trading tools and options education by options specialists.
- Provide account access via a variety of methods, such as computer, telephone, and Internet devices.
- Premium research and market News is provided by Goldman Sachs PrimeAccess, Standard and Poor's, Reuters, First Call, Briefing.com, and Ken Tower's Daily Market Commentary.

Minimal Computer Configuration

- Windows: XP Home or XP Professional.
- Processor: 2.5-GHz processor or faster.
- Random-access memory: at least 256 MB.
- Hard drive: 100 gigabytes.
- 19-inch monitor: 1024 × 728 16-bit color.
- Windows browser: Internet Explorer 6 or Mozilla Firefox 1.0 or higher.
- Recommended connection: T1, cable modem, or DSL. Do not use dial-up.

All copyrights and trademarks are the property of their respective owners.

Online Broker: E*Trade Financial Inc.

Company Web site: www.etrade.com

SUMMARY E*Trade is a progressive online discount broker that offers a diverse group of financial investment products for trading, investing, and banking. Its active trader services are aimed primarily at practiced active traders who are interested in using their knowledge of trading and taking advantage of discount pricing. E*Trade does not offer a simulator; therefore, an active trader must have a solid trading strategy in place and have experience with other online trading simulators before attempting to use E*Trade. Such practice can be gained at other online brokers, but it will not apply directly to using E*Trade; therefore, only seasoned active traders should consider using E*Trade.

Online technical support is available at an 800 number and by e-mail. E*Trade does not offer online seminars or workshops to help beginning active traders. E*Trade does provide free basic research on U.S. markets and global markets, news, streaming quotes, charts, stocks, options, and futures. The bonds and IPO center are subscriber fee-based. Refer to the company Web site for additional information.

The following material contains excerpts from the www.etrade. com Web site.

For Active Traders

SELECTED SOFTWARE FEATURES

*Power E*TRADE*
- Customizable no-fee active trader platform
- Trailing stops and bracketed and reserve orders
- Dedicated active trader service team
- Expanded 2-second execution guarantee, including ETFs
- Real-time intraday profit and loss tracker, streaming charts, and news
- Exclusive cash management tools and features for active traders

Options Trading Features
- Options strategies in IRAs and streaming options chains.
- Advanced options chains and analytics.
- Comprehensive options education from the Options Industry Council and the CBOE.
- Streaming real-time options.
- Buy calls and puts or sell cash-secured puts with level options trading.
- Level 2 and level 3 options trading available in IRAs.

Minimal Computer Configuration
- Windows: XP Home or XP Professional.
- Processor: 2.5-GHz processor or faster.
- Random-access Memory: at least 256 MB.
- Hard drive: 100 gigabytes.
- 19-inch monitor: 1024 × 728 16-bit color.
- Windows browser: Internet Explorer 6 or Mozilla Firefox 1.0 or higher.
- Recommended connection: T1, cable modem, or DSL. Do not use dial-up.

All copyrights and trademarks are the property of their respective owners.

Online Broker: Ameritrade Inc.

Company Web site: www.ameritrade.com

SUMMARY   Ameritrade offers a group of online applications for active traders to use in tracking market trends in real time and executing trades. Apex is the flagship online application for active traders. Ameritrade offers a variety of free services for an active trader after an account is opened. Ameritrade users must be familiar with online trading before using Ameritrade because Apex does not have a simulator or demo available. Therefore, active traders must have a solid trading strategy in place and experience with using other online trading simulators before attempting to use Ameritrade services.

Such practice can be gained from other online brokers, but it will not substitute for using Ameritrade. Demos are available on Ameritrade Streamer, Advanced Analyzer, QuoteScope, Command Center, SnapTicket, TradeTriggers, and options trading. These demos are very helpful in explaining how to use Ameritrade services, but they are not simulators of actual trading. Online technical support is available at an 800 number and by e-mail. Ameritrade does not offer online seminars or workshops to help beginning active traders. Refer to the company Web site for additional information.

The following material contains excerpts from the www. ameritrade.com Web site.

For Active Traders

SELECTED SOFTWARE FEATURES

Ameritrade Apex   Apex is used by active traders to manage and execute online trading activity. Apex is a fee-based service. However, after one becomes a customer, Ameritrade offers access to a group of free and useful active trading tools. Commissions and exception fees are charged.

Advanced Analyzer   Features include the ability to track, chart, and conduct research for trend spotting. Advanced Analyzer is free after one becomes an Ameritrade customer. Fees apply after 30 days.

Options Trading   Ameritrade accounts permit consideration of numerous options trading strategies. When this is combined with real-time streaming data, an active trader is able to address market opportunities effectively. Options trading is a fee-based service. The following Ameritrade services are free to Ameritrade customers:

Ameritrade Streamer   Ameritrade Streamer continuously monitors the market based on streaming quotes and other real-time information. Level 2 options quotes and alerts are available.

QuoteScope QuoteScope presents visualization of market data, enabling an active trader to measure liquidity changes.

Trade Triggers Trade Triggers is a unique function that permits an active trader to set alerts or place orders in advance when the market meets preestablished criteria.

Minimal Computer Configuration
- Windows: XP Home or XP Professional.
- Processor: 2.5-GHz processor or faster.
- Random-access memory: at least 256 MB.
- Hard drive: 100 gigabytes.
- 19-inch monitor: 1024 × 728 16-bit color.
- Windows Browser: Internet Explorer 6 or Mozilla Firefox 1.0 or higher.
- Recommended connection: T1, cable modem, or DSL. Do not use dial-up.

All copyrights and trademarks are the property of their respective owners.

Online Broker: Fidelity Investments Inc.

Company Web site: www.fidelity.com

The firm has offices in major cities. We have all had positive experiences with the Wilmette, Illinois, office.

SUMMARY Fidelity offers a variety of financial services and investment products. It also provides a dynamic online set of tools that enable everyone from a novice to an expert active trader to understand and develop trading skills. Fidelity offers two main products for active traders: Active Trader Pro and Wealth-Lab Pro. Both products have limits on trial period use; afterward fees are applied.

Active Trader Pro was created for a spectrum of users, from the beginner, to the intermediate, to the expert active trader. Active Trader Pro presents the most current market data in a uniquely defined user interface, allowing for personalization.

The Wealth-Lab Pro™ Technical Trading Platform also is designed for a spectrum of users from the beginner to the accomplished active trader for creating, back testing, and executing trading strategies. It has a very sophisticated staff and a first-class fixed-income desk.

Online technical support is available at an 800 number and by e-mail. Fidelity has online active trader events and newsletters to help beginning active traders. Refer to the company Web site for additional information.

The following material contains excerpts from the www.fidelity. com Web site.

For Active Traders

SELECTED SOFTWARE FEATURES

Fidelity Active Trader Pro
- Provides current market information in customizable layouts.
- Is able to place multiple trade order entry, trailing stop-loss orders, conditional orders, one-click trading, and skip-order previews.
- Place trailing stop-limit dollar or percentage trades good for the day or good until canceled.
- Directed trading offers an integrated streaming of time and sales data, including consolidated quotes from the NYSE, Nasdaq, SuperMontage, ARCA, BRUT, and INET.

- Eligible customers get level II quotes, time and sales, and watch lists.
- Has the ability to chart stocks, mutual funds, and indexes over specified time periods, such as intraday, for comparison to market and sector indexes or other securities.
- Research data provided by Lehman Brothers, Standard and Poor's, I-Watch, and Second Opinion.

Fidelity Wealth-Lab Pro
- Programming functions serve to create, back test, and execute customized trading strategies.
- Provides access to over 1,000 chart scripts and technical indicators for analysis purposes.

Minimal Computer Configuration
- Windows: XP Home or XP Professional.
- Processor: 2.5-GHz processor or faster.
- Random-access memory: at least 256 MB.
- Hard drive: 100 gigabytes.
- 19-inch monitor: 1024 × 728 16-bit color.
- Windows browser: Internet Explorer 6 or Mozilla Firefox 1.0 or higher.
- Recommended connection: T1, cable modem, or DSL. Do not use dial-up.

All the copyrights and trademarks are the property of their respective owners.

Trader's Notebook 5

Web Sites for Traders

Minimum Activity  Maximum Activity

0   1   2   3   4   5   6   7   8

What follows is a list of Web sites to assist you in your trading research. A variety of price points and content are represented that provide the depth of research needed for all levels of investors and traders, from the amateur to the professional. We offer reviews of some of the sites and provide merely a reference point for others. Taken as a whole, this gives the reader a good cross-section of the available sites across the vast World Wide Web. Some, such as *The Wall Street Journal* and the television networks, you already are familiar with. Others, such as the economy.com site and Grant's, may be new to many of you. Some are more proprietary in nature, such as Ameritrade. You will find many sites that cover the equity markets quite well. You will find far fewer that cover the futures markets and fewer still that cover both.

There are far too many brokerage firms to mention them all, and so I have limited the list to a very few. Stock brokerage firms generally handle all stocks. However, in the futures business, there are a lot of firms that handle only a limited numbers of instruments, eliminating spreads, agricuturals, or even some of the financials. Often these firms have a bottom-level price but no service or research. If you are using one of these firms, you may miss out on a move if they do not handle the appropriate instrument and what they do handle is not moving in a predictable direction. We have not covered the pure charting services, since that is solely a price and preference decision on your part, and we would prefer to keep an arm's-length distance from that area.

Barron's Online

www.barrons.com

Barron's Online is the sister publication to *The Wall Street Journal* and is available to WSJ Interactive subscribers at no additional charge. It is also available separately for those who do not choose to use WSJ. Barron's weekly format allows for more in-depth coverage of its subject matter. Both are similarly organized and easy to navigate. However, be forewarned that both Barron's and WSJ carry the bias of the Dow Jones organization. Although it is useful to know what that bias is, it may not have universal utility. The publication *Barron's* is useful, however, and is a must read for all investors.

Bloomberg

www.bloomberg.com

One of the premium sites for investing and economic news, this site provides a combination of paid and free resources. The site is well thought out and easy to navigate. The information provided is of great value to serious investors. This organization was built on the flow of information in and out of Wall Street. The site not only covers equities, which normally are covered by most sites, but also does a thorough job of covering currencies and commodities, which seem to get short shrift at most sites. The company made its reputation by providing sophisticated data and trading news feeds to professionals. In a sense, this Web site is a lighter-duty view of what is offered at much higher prices in the direct feeds.

Ameritrade

www.ameritrade.com

This is a former Big Easy investor site that has been bought by Ameritrade. Big Easy investor provides the data and charting and screening power behind the site. However, the meat of the site is the presentation and availability of downloadable software for analyzing and screening stocks. Many of the site links may seem trivial to a seasoned investor; they are there to assist the neophyte. The software appears to be well written and easy to use and provides the researcher with a myriad of information on which to base investment decisions. Training materials are supplied to make the learning curve as short and painless as possible. Extensive screening devices can provide an investor with self-defined or prepackaged screens that can be used to custom build portfolios to suit the individual. There is also a facility for sending charts via e-mail as .gif files so that information can be shared easily between investors. The charge is $20 per month, including daily data updates, and it is coupled to an Ameritrade account.

Navigating the software is as easy as point and click. Complete charting and analysis tools are readily at hand for researching the characteristics of individual equities. There is access to press releases and even a device to make contact with other investors to obtain their opinions. Numerous criteria are available for screening, and so a good fit into a portfolio can be engineered.

The Bull Market Report

www.bullmarket.com

The Bull Market Report is a daily subscription-based e-mail newsletter. The objective of the newsletter and the news flashes and support data available at the Web site is to find the best wealth creation securities for the next decade. Portfolios are maintained and watched in the following areas: business-to-business: broadband, data communications, Internet, drug and biotech, financial services, and wireless. Additionally, there is an aggressive growth portfolio and a long-term core holdings portfolio. Although these are investment portfolios composed of elements from the other, smaller portfolios, the smaller specific portfolios serve as trading springboards to the investment program. Using this two-tier approach, future leaders are tested at the trading level before they reach the status of an investment vehicle.

The statistical data that go into the analysis of these securities are available at the Web site. This is an approach designed to beat the market consistently. Since this program is under constant scrutiny, positions are adjusted regularly to match the required criteria. The Web site is quite user-friendly, and with its uncluttered look, navigation is swift.

CNBC.com

www.moneycentral.msn.com

CNBC.com is now a part of the Microsoft empire in that it is part of the MSN Money Central site, as indicated by the link shown above. The CNBC Web site gives direct access to its daylong market programming via the computer. Although the site is fairly easy to navigate, bear in mind the extreme bias of the information coming out of this major media service. A contrarian approach should be considered in assimilating most of the information presented. Remember, by the very nature of its business, CNBC is obligated to fill the airwaves every second of the broadcast day whether or not something newsworthy is occurring. This drifts over to the Web site, where at times some of the information appears somewhat trivial.

There are extensive articles of interest, most of which are well written. Contributors to CNBC are many, but there is usually a vested interest through advertising, and so the general scope is somewhat narrow. The bias is clearly mainline Wall Street, and stock picks reflect this. Company analyses are of good quality, competitive with those of other services. This site gives you a glimpse of current events as they unfold, and that serves as a good source of background information. Financial decisions, however, need to be based on more in-depth analysis, which is outside the scope of this service. For that purpose, raw data, charting, and unbiased analysis are required.

This is an important resource for purposes of reading the market pulse. However, it should not be relied on as a domicile of market mavens. CNBC guests do not get on the station by accident. There are public relations firms that are specialists at placing stories and guests on the right station. In fact, the author worked at such a firm while attending Northwestern University in Evanston, Illinois.

The Dismal Scientist

www.economy.com

This is a part of the economy.com complex and is accessible through it. *Dismal Scientist* provides a thorough look at the global macroeconomic situation. It is a for-pay newsletter for investing and economic professionals.

Grant's Online

www.grantspub.com

This is the Web site for www.grantspub.com, the publisher of *Grant's Interest Rate Observer*. The *Interest Rate Observer* is one of the focused publications from Grant's Financial Publications. Although these publications are geared to the financial professional and the pricey subscription rates reflect it, they contain information that can be beneficial to any investor. The *Interest Rate Observer* targets issues and investment opportunities in the global interest rate and currency markets. It points out differences between varying nations and how those differences can create cross-national investment opportunities. The analyses can assist a researcher in determining the direction and relationship of global interest rate movements and their effect on the bond and currency markets. In addition to the articles in the hard copies of the *Interest Rate Observer*, Grant's online makes back issues of the publication available, provides market analysis and commentary, markets books and merchandise, and includes a cartoon treasury of financially correct cover cartoons by Hank Blaustein.

This is a publication with a point of view. *Grant's* does not necessarily follow the line of the Street. Instead, it attempts to identify change where it occurs most frequently: at the margin. In comparison to the postulations of the brokerage houses and the media, the approach is fresh and at times irreverent, eclipsing the thousands of newsletters flooding the market.

Grant's is unique, and with its focus being so tight, the writing is knowledgeable and any conclusions drawn from it carry with them the assurance of being based on sound judgment. Although the site and some of its areas are free, this is not a totally free service, and accessing some of the articles and areas carries a price. This is a site that is worth checking out. (They also have an e-mail service to notify subscribers and nonsubscribers alike of the presence of new material.) Enough free information is given for the reader to determine whether more in-depth fee-based information is needed for a specific area of research. Abstracts assist researchers in determining the subjects covered and their relevance.

The material presented is sophisticated and geared toward the serious professional who needs insight into the interest rate and financial markets. Although a less experienced investor may profit from some of the material presented, as a whole, this service would be overkill for most individuals. For a serious professional, this should be considered a key research resource.

INO.com

www.ino.com

INO.com is a service that Focuses on the futures industry. Although there is some information on the equity markets, the strongest emphasis is on futures, and this is shown by the fact that links and sponsors are primarily in the futures industry. Charts, technical analysis, and trading strategies are made available. There is also a free daily e-mail service that posts end-of-day summaries, extreme movements in markets, pertinent news, and headlines. Once you weed out the extensive advertising, you will find information that is for the most part of reasonable value.

In addition to the various free sites, premium services are available for more sophisticated levels of research and more detailed and personalized charting. The interactive discussion groups also can be of interest. This is a full-service site for futures and options traders. Although all the information may not prove to be useful, some of it will, and this should be a readily visited address. Get the e-mail alerts.

MarketMavens.com

www.marketmavens.com

The *Market Mavens Report* is a publication of Pinson Communications of Clearwater, Florida. It is an inexpensive service, costing $60 per year. It has a free subscriber e-mail service that allows investors to obtain timely information on an alert basis. Updates of material are done on a regular daily basis, covering 39 investment sectors and drawing on the expertise of 50 investment analysts. There are also numerous links to other investment resources, including www.traderspress.com. The site contains articles, generally well written, on the subjects listed above, varying from the most serious to the more frivolous. It is a site worth visiting as you perform your analysis of a specific asset before making an investment. Since new articles are posted daily, regular viewing of the site, along with the support of the alert service, is bound to turn up some insight that will prove profitable for both technicians and fundamentalists. This is a general service investment site, but for the most part it is packed with salient information. For those so inclined, there is even a section on the astrological aspects of investing.

The site has an appeal to the individual investor and the professional alike and provides information on the entire investment sector. There is such a wealth of information available that no individual will need to scan the entire site but instead can focus on specific areas of interest and specific contributing authors. There is information at this site that can benefit all levels of investors. This site provides reasonable one-stop access to the investment opinions and research of key analysts throughout the industry. Quality and depth of analysis vary with the writers and their points of view and the intended target audience. There is no particular bias at this site; so many analysts are represented that the full investment spectrum is covered. Experience in using the site will reveal to a researcher which areas are most useful to that individual.

An excellent way to keep abreast of what *Market Mavens* is doing is to get on its free e-mail alert list so that one can get a daily overview of the site. You will find some material useful to your needs and can ignore the rest. The site is too expansive for all the articles to have universal appeal.

Morningstar.com

www.morningstar.com

Morningstar's focus is the analysis of mutual funds. This Web site carries on that focus and gives the individual investor access to its rating system and analyses. However, be aware that there is bias here, and you may not always agree with the ratings or the rationale behind them. Although this is a valuable resource for fund investors and traders, it should not be their only resource. Knowledge of the investments that make up the fund is of great importance and should be a part of any research program in equities.

Morningstar fund analyses are among the most widely quoted in the industry. At the Web site, there is a clear extension beyond fund analysis, and the entire bond and equity market is covered. The fact that this mainline firm also touts contrarian investing is refreshing. Morningstar staffers present meaningful information. As would be expected, there is less reliance on outside advisers since Morningstar is an advisory and research firm.

There is much of value available at this site in both the mutual fund and equity businesses.

Optimainvestor.com

www.optimainvestor.com

Optimainvestor.com is a fee-based research source for the futures and equity markets that currently is priced at $295 per month. The layout of its pages makes it clear, easy to use, and uncluttered. The fee includes a daily e-mail service that leads the user to pertinent information and also presents daily trading recommendations. The price is considerably higher than that of most sites, but the quality and reliability of the information justify the pricing.

The owner of the firm used to be in the bond pit, and so you are getting information from someone who has been there and done that, as the expression goes. A nice feature: Unlike most services, you can talk to them on the phone.

This is a key resource in the arsenal of a professional trader.

economy.com

www.economy.com

Economy.com is geared to serious professionals. It offers thorough, current research on the U.S. macroeconomy; the economies of states, metropolitan areas, and industries; and certain key international economies. The in-detail studies are fee-based. Information is available on 315 metropolitan areas and 32 industries in the consumer, health services, financial, and business services sectors. This is a new service, and expansion of its scope is anticipated. Historical and forecast reports are available for all 50 states plus Puerto Rico and the District of Columbia. Equally thorough coverage of Canada is included at this time.

Economy.com also publishes detailed historical and forecast reports on 100 occupations in the covered metro areas and states. Recent performance tables provide an efficient means of updating the information in the reports. There is also analysis of employment figures and various other product listings.

derivatives.com

www.appliederivatives.com

There are three publications involved here. All are published on the Web only by Patrick Young of London, England. *Appliederivatives. com* and its sister publication *eriviatives.com* are free monthly magazines that are published on the Web and offer news and tidbits about the futures industry worldwide, its people, and its exchanges. There is also a subscriber-based interactive service that is just coming online. This trio of publications provides a good view of the futures industry, particularly the political side.

The Kirk Report

www.thekirkreport.com

This is a news and investment site presented by an individual investor who makes his living from equities and shares his trials, tribulations, and methods of success publicly on the site. His recommendations hit the mark most of the time, and it is good reading as well. The site is best for the individual stock investor, not necessarily for the heavy-duty professional, as it is somewhat light-duty.

The Wall Street Journal

www.wsj.com

Regular subscribers to the daily *Wall Street Journal* have the option of adding the Internet-based interactive edition for an annual fee of $29. This gives the subscriber the entire text of the daily edition plus access to back issues, additional articles and news flashes, and links to other resources, including the other Dow Jones publications, such as *Barron's*. As things happen during the day, an e-mail alert service is available so that the subscriber can get instant notice of important events, such as an analysis of a Federal Open Market Committee meeting or key market swings or corporate announcements. During eventful days on Wall Street, these alerts come through on a regular basis and give the reader the option of going into greater depth, taking action on the basis of the release, or ignoring it. Navigating the site is as easy as clicking on the links that send you through the publication. The information available is what would be expected from a major newspaper and does carry its own bias.

I would not recommend that anyone rely on this site as his or her sole source of information but would recommend that it be a part of a trader's menu of regular readings. In any research project, the opinions of the major players in the media must carry some weight, but a balance must be struck between that and more focused reporting from sources that are closer to the market or are known for their courage of contrary opinion. The market does not necessarily head where the media say it is headed, but it most certainly has been there. Market psychology is complex, and it takes a diversity of resource information to decipher it.

If you find value in *The Wall Street Journal*, you will enjoy working with this site, since it contains much of the same information. For the computer-bound, it has the convenience of being onscreen or just a click away, with the additional convenience of sending you to complementary information to maintain continuity in your research. The interactive edition can serve as an aid in working with the print version, as it does an effective job of encapsulating subject matter so that the reader can choose whether to proceed to the full article in the print version or remain online. WSJ Online is available as a stand-alone product for about $80.

NumaWeb

www.numa.com

What are derivatives? How are they used? They're very risky aren't they? These questions and others can be answered at www.numa.com. NumaWeb is the Internet home page for financial derivatives. Visitors to numa.com will find a wealth of information on derivative markets and the derivative industry, along with reference material. Comments on the derivative market and price data can be found by visiting an exchange from a list of over 60 exchanges worldwide.

To keep browsing easy, the home page provides many links. Numa.com has a link to the largest database of financial courses and conferences at www.financialconference.com. Other links include news groups and chat forums. In the chat forums comments on topics, including derivatives, are encouraged and related questions are answered.

For industry professionals, the site provides a free derivative announcement service. This service allows the industry to get in touch with the site's over 2,500 visitors each week. For the reader, the site also includes a bookshop with over 1,600 investment-related books in its catalogue. A list of derivative software companies, along with products and contacts, is also on www.numa.com. If industry professionals are offering or looking for employment, NumaWeb has a few free bulletin boards of derivative-related jobs.

NumaWeb also has research-related material on its Web site. The option strategy guide can help you find the most appropriate option strategy for any particular market view. The guide includes very clear profit and loss profiles for 17 option strategies. Option traders can find option calculators for options, multiple options, convertible bonds, and warrants. NumaWeb has a guide to entering futures and option orders as well as derivative Internet links to glossaries.

For end users one of the most difficult challenges on the Web is finding the sites they want. NumaWeb addresses this problem for the derivatives industry. The site provides links to all derivative information that is not included on the home page. What impressed me most about the site is that the user can be notified by e-mail when there are any significant additions to the site. Although the Web site is not visually stimulating, it can answer any derivative-related questions you have.

Note: This site was reviewed by Eric Redden, a student in a class on fundamental analysis at the CME.

Seeking Alpha

www.seekingalpha.com

This is the only site reviewed here that directs you to investment and finance blogs. There is a wealth of information here, with something of use to every level of user. It is a good starting place for any research project and can serve as a launch pad to other sites, as many of the other sites discussed here are available as links through this blog.

These following Web sites, which were used in the preparation of this report, may be useful in your trading:

www.investorlinks.com
www.cbsmarketwatch.com
www.lowrisk.com
www.strasser.com
www.yahoo.com
www.motherjones.com
www.derivitives.com
www.bobbrinker.com
www.clearstation.com
www.equityalert.com
www.financialengines.com
www.stocktrak.com
www.mrci.com
www.foxnews.com
www.nbc.com
www.abc.com
www.futurespartners.com
www.msn.com

For day-to-day coverage of the markets on a news basis, consider John Lothian's newsletter. Yes, I read it.

There are some great money management sites. Get a free list from Tom Dangelo at manusrisco.com.

For Forex trading, you can practice on a simulator.

There is a free course on trading the foreign exchange market waiting for you. Visit the Chicago Mercantile Exchange at CME.com and go to the education center.

From time to time, I check with Dave Landry's column. He can be reached at Tradingmarkets.com.

Currenly, I have a subscription to the *Financial Times,* and *The New York Times.* Both have suberb business sections. Add to that the facilities of the Globex Learning Center and Information Center and it's a wonder I have time to trade.

If you trade the E-mini, check out E-minimaster.com. Jim Harrison does a great job of phone coaching: 972-200-5014. Unfortunately, Jim lives in Dallas.

Trader's Notebook 6

If You Want to Know the Markets, Know the Reports

Minimum Activity  Maximum Activity

0   1   2   3   4   5   6   7   8

Which government reports are really important? It depends on the markets you trade. In a survey of 14 analysts, the following were considered most important when one is looking at the general health of the economy.

Oil futures: the current price of a barrel of oil
ISM Index: a monthly gauge of the manufacturing sector
Jobless claims: a weekly tally of unemployment
Foreign currencies: the value of the dollar compared with that of other currencies
10-year Treasuries: measure the cost of borrowing

However, if you see auto sales falling along with consumer confidence, it means you should get out of the market. That was the lethal combination that triggered the crash of 1929.

Today's active trader should have some notion of how often and when many reports hit the media. Stocks, bonds, and currencies bounce around, adjusting to economic statistics. These numbers are released when the market is active. Add testimony by the Fed's chair and you have a formula for active fireworks.

It would be beneficial to have a monthly calendar on your desk. You can print one out by using the following outline resource: www.fidweek.econoday.com. They offer a service for as little as $75 per year. Or go to nber.org/releases/.

Of course, there is plenty of information at Bloomberg, MarketWatch, Money.cnn, and Yahoo! There are financial newspapers that make economic reports available. The key thing to remember is that these reports are consumed, digested, and then regurgitated in minutes over the financial networks. Know which reports influence your markets.

If you are a short-term active trader, you must be aware of reports. For those with a longer time horizon, these reports are less significant.

Trader's Notebook 7

Trading Spreads

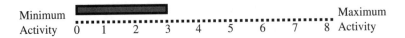

Minimum Activity   0   1   2   3   4   5   6   7   8   Maximum Activity

This chapter gives you a short course in spreads. The author would like to thank Gecko software for its contribution.

What Are Spreads?

The futures markets provide a variety of trading opportunities. In addition to profiting from rising prices by purchasing futures contracts and profiting from falling prices by selling those contracts, there is an opportunity to profit from the relationship between different contracts—or the *spread*. A spread refers to the simultaneous purchase and sale of two or more different but related futures contracts in the expectation that a profit will be made when the position is offset.

Examples include buying one futures contract and selling another futures contract on the same commodity but with a different delivery month, buying and selling the same delivery month on different exchanges, and buying a delivery month of one futures contract and selling the same delivery month (or close to it) of a different but related futures contract.

When establishing, or "putting on," a spread, a trader looks at the price differential of the spread rather than the absolute price levels. The contract that is viewed as "cheap" is purchased, or a long position is established. The contract that is viewed as "expensive" is sold, or a short position is established. If market prices move as expected, meaning that the long position gains in value relative to the short position, the trader profits from the change in the relationship between the prices. The concern for a spread trader is the change in the relationship between the contract on which he or she is long and the one on which he or she is short. For example, assume that a trader is buying July (establishing a long position) CBOT wheat and selling (establishing a short position) December CBOT wheat. The trader will profit from this position if any of the following occur:

1. The long contract increases in value more than the short contract does. For example, if over the course of a week, July CBOT wheat increases in value 15 cents a bushel ($750 before commissions and fees) and December CBOT wheat increases in value only 10 cents a bushel ($500 before commissions and fees), the spread trader in this position has a profit of 5 cents a bushel ($250 before commissions and fees) because the long position gained 15 cents a bushel and the short position lost 10 cents a bushel.

   P&L: +15 cents (+$750) − 10 cents (−$500) + 5 cents (+$250)

2. The long contract decreases in value less than the short contract does. For example, if over the course of a week, July CBOT wheat decreases in value by 10 cents a bushel (−$500 before commissions and fees) and December CBOT wheat decreases in value 15 cents a bushel (−$750 before commissions and fees), the spread trader in this position has a profit of 5 cents a bushel, even though both contracts declined.

   P&L: −10 cents (−$500) + 15 cents (+$750) + 5 cents (+$250)

3. The long contract increases in value and the short contract decreases in value. For example, if July CBOT wheat gains 2 cents per bushel (+$100 before commissions and fees) and December CBOT wheat decreases by 3 cents a bushel (+$150 before commissions and fees because the trader is short), the spread trader in this position has a profit of 5 cents a bushel, as he or she gained on both sides of the spread trade.

P&L: +2 cents (+$100) − 3 cents (+$150) + 5 cents (+$250)

Remember, the concern for a spread trader is the change in the relationship between the contract he or she is long and the contract he or she is short, not the absolute price level of the commodity in question. For example, reexamine case 2 above, in which the contract on which the trader was long decreased in value by $500. However, because the contract on which the spread trader was short decreased in value by $750, resulting in a gain of $750 before commissions and fees, the spread trader ended up making money because the long contract gained in value relative to the short position. Of course, spread trading is not guaranteed to eliminate trading losses. If the long contract decreases in value relative to the short position, the spread trader will incur losses. Let's assume the same position as in the example above: A spread trader is buying July (long) CBOT wheat and selling (short) December CBOT wheat. The trader will incur losses from this position if any of the following things occur:

1. The long contract increases in value less than the short contract does. For example, if over the course of a week, July CBOT wheat increases in value 10 cents a bushel ($500 before commissions and fees) and December CBOT wheat increases in value 15 cents a bushel ($750 before commissions and fees), the spread trader in this position has a loss of 5 cents a bushel (−$250 before commissions and fees)

because the long position gained only 10 cents a bushel whereas the short position lost 15 cents a bushel.

P&L: +10 cents (+$500) − 15 cents (−$750) − 15 cents (−$250)

2. The long contract decreases in value more than the short contract does. For example, if over the course of a week, July CBOT wheat decreases in value by 15 cents a bushel (−$750 before commissions and fees) and December CBOT wheat decreases in value by only 10 cents a bushel (−$500 before commissions and fees), the spread trader in this position has a loss of 5 cents a bushel.

P&L: −15 cents (−$750) + 10 cents (+$500) − 5 cents (−$250)

The key to spread trading is the relative performance of one futures contract to another. Though some spreads have a basic market bias—these are known as bull and bear spreads—the absolute price level of the underlying commodity contracts is not important, only the relative performance of one contract versus the other. In other words, a spread trade is a speculation that one contract will outperform another contract.

Why Trade Spreads?

Spread trading, like any other form of speculation, is not for everybody. Trading spreads is very different from the short-term hit-and-run trading most outright futures traders do.

The main reasons most professional traders state for trading spreads are

Lower risk
Attractive margin rates
Increased predictability

Because of their hedged nature, spreads generally are less risky than outright futures positions. Most professional traders who trade spreads usually cite this as the number one reason for trading spreads. Since the prices of two different futures contracts (on the same commodity or different but related commodities) exhibit a strong tendency to move up or down together, spread trading offers protection against losses that arise from unexpected or extreme price volatility.

Not all spreads have lower risk than outright futures positions. For example, "old crop" versus "new crop" grain spreads may exhibit equal or even greater risk.

However, careful examination of the spreads you are considering should yield a stable of spreads that tend to have lower risk characteristics. This can help lower the volatility of the market you are trading and reduce the fluctuations in your trading account.

Spreads offer "protection" because losses on one side of the spread are offset more or less by gains from the other side of the spread. For example, if the short (sell) side of a spread results in a loss because of an increase in price, the long (buy) side of the spread probably will produce a profit, offsetting much, if not all, of the loss.

Spread trading does have risks, but generally, because of the partially hedged nature of spreads, they tend to exhibit lower risk in general. In most cases, the least risky spreads are intramarket (delivery) spreads, followed by intermarket (interexchange) spreads and then intercommodity spreads.

As a result of the partially hedged nature of spread positions, spread margins tend to be margined at a lower rate than are outright futures positions. Like any other margin requirement, spread margin minimum levels are set by the exchanges and can be higher, depending on your brokerage house. Spread margins are subject to change without notice by either your brokerage house or the exchange, just like any other margin level.

Because of the generally lower margin levels charged for spreads, traders are able to trade a larger variety of positions, increasing their diversification. Also, because of the lower margin rates, which are a function of volatility, spreads allow traders to risk a smaller percentage of their capital on any single trade.

Margin levels for spreads can be used as a rough guide for the level of risk involved in a particular market. Generally, the higher the margin rate is, the higher the risk involved in trading that particular market is, along with a higher potential reward. Thus, spread traders usually choose this avenue because of the lower perceived risks and are willing to sacrifice the tremendous upside potential of trading straight futures positions in return for the lower risk of trading spreads.

Most spread traders feel that spreads are more predictable than outright futures positions. Some of this predictability may be due to the lower risk involved in spreads. With lower volatility, it is easier for traders to take advantage of longer-term price moves, as the lower volatility makes it easier for them to ride out corrections within major trends instead of being shaken out of a position on those corrections, as often happens to straight futures traders.

Also, spreads are much less sensitive to sudden shocks to a market, such as an unforeseen news event. Because of this, many traders feel they are more predictable. Another commonly stated reason for their increased predictability is the greater liquidity in most spread markets. Whereas many markets may be good for 50 or 100 contracts at any price that bid or offered, it is not uncommon to see spread trading in the same market good for 500 to 1,000 spreads. The spread markets are generally extremely liquid, and many traders feel they offer a better opportunity than outright futures positions.

Finally, some traders feel that spread markets are more predictable because they are off the beaten path. Thousands of systems have been developed for trading futures. Therefore, some of the strong tendencies of the markets have shifted because they have become so popular and well known. However, spread trading still is considered much too complicated or esoteric for many, and many of these market anomalies have not been worked out of the market.

Though no one knows for sure if spreads really are more predictable, traders find that spreads tend to trend well. Also, because of the high liquidity in the spread markets, they tend to chart and hold support or resistance levels very well.

Ironically, some of the very qualities of spread trading cited as benefits by the pros are perceived as a drawbacks by non-professionals.

Many people cite the slower movement and lower volatility of the spread markets as drawbacks. Spreads do not tend to offer the excitement of "in and out" straight futures trading.

The general lack of risk also means that the potential rewards are smaller. Risk and reward almost always occur in direct relation to each other. Therefore, the partially hedged nature of spreads, which tends to limit risk (reduce volatility), also tends to cause profits to be smaller. In other words, several traders describe spread trading as being about as exciting as watching grass grow.

Another drawback of trading spreads is the double commission structure. Remember, spreads involve two different futures contracts, and thus there is double the cost of trading. Commissions in the futures market generally are charged on a per-contract basis.

Therefore, trading a spread involves twice the cost of trading outright futures positions.

Speculators need to consider commissions when running their own trading businesses. Commissions are a cost, plain and simple. In trading spreads, this cost is higher. In fact, it is often said that brokers invented spreads so that they could charge double commissions. Though traders cannot ignore this cost, they can work on reducing it. Often, many brokerage firms will charge a lower rate on a per-contract basis for spread trades. Though this "spread commission" is still typically higher than the cost of trading an outright (single contract) position, it is often less than double the existing single contract position rate.

Trader's Notebook 8

Free Financial Education

Minimum Activity 0 1 2 3 4 5 6 7 8 Maximum Activity

Bob Brinker has been the host of *Money Talk* for over 20 years. His three-hour radio show is the best place for conservative investing and trading advice. I've listed the radio stations below for your convenience. When I teach, I expect the students to find the appropriate station. This time I will make an exception.

Note that I am not affiliated with the program or with ABC. If you are new to investing, you must become a listener. If you cannot receive the station, they have a feature called "Money Talk on Demand." This is the best bargain for a solid foundation in trading.

State	Market(s)	Station	Frequency
Alabama	Anniston	WDNG	1450 AM
Alabama	Athens	WVNN	770 AM
Alabama	Brewton	WEBJ	1240 AM
Alabama	Dothan	WWNT	1450 AM
Alabama	Florence	WBCF	1240 AM
Alabama	Mobile	WABB	1480 AM
Alabama	Guntersville	WGSV	1270 AM

State	Market(s)	Station	Frequency
Alaska	Anchorage	KENI	650 AM
Alaska	Fairbanks	KFAR	660 AM
Alaska	Soldotna	KSRM	920 AM
Arizona	Phoenix	KFNN	1510 AM
Arizona	Tucson	KNST	790 AM
Arkansas	Farmington	KFAY	1030 AM
Arkansas	Hot Springs	KZNG	1340 AM
California	Bakersfield	KERN	1410 AM
California	Chico	KPAY	1290 AM
California	Eureka	KGOE	1480 AM
California	Grass Valley	KNCO	830 AM
California	Lake Isabella	KQAB	1140 AM
California	Lompoc	KTME	1410 AM
California	Los Angeles	KABC	790 AM
California	Palm Springs	KPSI	920 AM
California	Sacramento	KFBK	1530 AM
California	San Francisco	KGO	810 AM
California	San Francisco	KTRB	860 AM
California	Santa Barbara	KIST	1340 AM
California	Santa Maria	KUHL	1440 AM
California	Susanville	KSUE	1240 AM
Colorado	Colorado Springs	KVOR	740 AM
Colorado	Cortez	KVFC	740 AM
Colorado	Denver	KNUS	710 AM
Colorado	Durango	KDGO	1240 AM
Colorado	Greeley	KFKA	1310 AM
Colorado	Pueblo	KCSJ	590 AM

(*Continued*)

State	Market(s)	Station	Frequency
Connecticut	Hartford	WTIC	1080 AM
Connecticut	Norwalk	WNLK	1350 AM
Connecticut	Stamford	WSTC	1400 AM
Delaware	Rehoboth Beach	WGMD	92.7 FM
Florida	Brooksville	WWJB	1450 AM
Florida	Lake Placid	WWTK	730 AM
Florida	Lakeland	WLKF	1430 AM
Florida	Melbourne	WMEL	920 AM
Florida	Miami	WIOD	610 AM
Florida	Naples	WNOG	1270 AM
Florida	Pensacola	WCOA	1370 AM
Florida	Punta Gorda	WCCF	1580 AM
Florida	Sarasota	WLSS	930 AM
Florida	Springfield	WYOO	101.1 FM
Florida	St. Augustine	WFOY	1240 AM
Florida	Tampa	WHNZ	1250 AM
Florida	West Palm Beach	WBZT	1230 AM
Georgia	Savannah	WBMQ	630 AM
Hawaii	Honolulu	KHNR	97.5 FM
Idaho	Boise	KBOI	670 AM
Idaho	Twin Falls	KLIX	1310 AM
Illinois	Bloomington	WJBC	1230 AM
Illinois	Brookport	WNTX	750 AM
Illinois	Carbondale	WCIL	1020 AM
Illinois	Chicago	WLS	890 AM
Illinois	Decatur	WSOY	1340 AM
Illinois	Herrin	WJPF	1340 AM
Illinois	Peoria	WMBD	1470 AM
Illinois	Quincy	WGEM	105.1 FM

State	Market(s)	Station	Frequency
Illinois	Springfield	WMAY	970 AM
Indiana	Bloomington	WGCL	1370 AM
Iowa	Burlington	KCPS	1150 AM
Iowa	Cedar Rapids	WMT	600 AM
Iowa	Davenport	WOC	1420 AM
Iowa	Des Moines	WHO	1040 AM
Iowa	Fairfield	KMCD	1570 AM
Iowa	Sioux City	KMNS	620 AM
Iowa	Sioux City	KSCJ	1360 AM
Kansas	Holcomb	KBUF	1030 AM
Kansas	Topeka	KMAJ	1440 AM
Kansas	Wichita	KNSS	1330 AM
Kentucky	Glasgow	WCLU	1490 AM
Kentucky	Hopkinsville	WHOP	1230 AM
Louisiana	Abbeville	KPEL	105.1 FM
Louisiana	Baton Rouge	WJBO	1150 AM
Louisiana	New Orleans	WWL	870 AM
Maine	Boothbay Harbor	WCME	96.7 FM
Maine	Howland	WVOM	103.9 FM
Massachusetts	Boston	WRKO	680 AM
Massachusetts	West Yarmouth	WXTK	95.1 FM
Massachusetts	Worcester	WTAG	580 AM
Michigan	Alpena	WATZ	1450 AM
Michigan	Benton Harbor-St. Jo	WHFB	1060 AM
Michigan	Detroit	WJR	760 AM
Michigan	Grand Rapids	WOOD	1300 AM

(*Continued*)

State	Market(s)	Station	Frequency
Michigan	Kalamazoo	WKMI	1360 AM
Michigan	Lansing	WJIM	1240 AM
Michigan	Saginaw	WSGW	790 AM
Michigan	Traverse City	WTCM	580 AM
Minnesota	Alexandria	KXRA	1490 AM
Minnesota	East Grand Forks	KCNN	1590 AM
Minnesota	Hutchinson	KDUZ	1260 AM
Minnesota	St. Cloud	KNSI	1450 AM
Minnesota	Willmar	KWLM	1340 AM
Mississippi	Biloxi	WTNI	1640 AM
Mississippi	Cleveland	WDSK	1410 AM
Mississippi	Laurel	WMXI	98.1 FM
Mississippi	Pearl	WJNT	1180 AM
Missouri	Cape Girardeau	KZIM	960 AM
Missouri	Columbia	KFRU	1400 AM
Missouri	Farmington	KREI	800 AM
Missouri	Festus	KJFF	1400 AM
Missouri	Jefferson City	KWOS	950 AM
Missouri	Kansas City	KCMO	710 AM
Missouri	Poplar Bluff	KWOC	930 AM
Missouri	Sikeston	KSIM	1400 AM
Missouri	Springfield	KWTO	560 AM
Montana	Hardin	KHDN	1230 AM
Montana	Laurel	KBSR	1490 AM
Montana	Missoula	KYLT	1340 AM
Montana	Whitefish	KJJR	880 AM
Nebraska	Lincoln	KLIN	1400 AM

State	Market(s)	Station	Frequency
Nebraska	Omaha	KKAR	1290 AM
Nevada	North Las Vegas	KXNT	840 AM
Nevada	Reno	KKOH	780 AM
New Hampshire	Dover	WTSN	1270 AM
New Hampshire	Laconia	WEMJ	1490 AM
New Hampshire	New London	WNTK	99.7 FM
New Jersey	Princeton	WHWH	1350 AM
New Mexico	Alamogordo	KINN	1270 AM
New Mexico	Albuquerque	KKOB	770 AM
New York	Buffalo	WBEN	930 AM
New York	Cortland	WKRT	920 AM
New York	Horseheads	WWLZ	820 AM
New York	New York	WABC	770 AM
New York	Rochester	WHAM	1180 AM
New York	Schenectady	WGY	810 AM
New York	Utica	WIBX	950 AM
New York	Watertown	WTNY	790 AM
North Carolina	Black Mountain	WZNN	1350 AM
North Carolina	Charlotte	WBT	1110 AM
North Carolina	High Point	WMFR	1230 AM
North Carolina	Southern Pines	WEEB	990 AM
North Carolina	Washington	WDLX	930 AM
North Dakota	Bismarck	KFYR	550 AM
North Dakota	Fargo	WDAY	970 AM
Ohio	Bellaire	WOMP	1290 AM
Ohio	Canada	CHER	0 AM
Ohio	Mansfield	WMAN	1400 AM

(Continued)

State	Market(s)	Station	Frequency
Ohio	Marietta	WLTP	910 AM
Ohio	Steubenville	WSTV	1340 AM
Oregon	Bend	KBND	1110 AM
Oregon	Corvallis	KLOO	1340 AM
Oregon	Enterprise	KWVR	1340 AM
Oregon	Eugene	KUGN	590 AM
Oregon	Klamath Falls	KAGO	1150 AM
Oregon	Newport	KNPT	1310 AM
Oregon	Phoenix	KCMX	880 AM
Oregon	Portland	KXL	750 AM
Oregon	The Dalles	KACI	1300 AM
Pennsylvania	Altoona	WRTA	1240 AM
Pennsylvania	Erie	WJET	1400 AM
Pennsylvania	Harrisburg	WHP	580 AM
Pennsylvania	Hughesville	WRKK	1200 AM
Pennsylvania	Johnstown	WNTJ	850 AM
Pennsylvania	Somerset	WNTW	990 AM
Pennsylvania	Williamsport	WRAK	1400 AM
South Carolina	Charleston	WTMA	1250 AM
South Carolina	Chester	WBT	99.3 FM
South Carolina	Greenville	WYRD	1330 AM
South Carolina	Socastee	WRNN	99.5 FM
South Carolina	Spartanburg	WORD	950 AM
South Dakota	Sioux Falls	KSOO	1140 AM
Tennessee	Memphis	KWAM	990 AM
Texas	Abilene	KSLI	1280 AM
Texas	Amarillo	KIXZ	940 AM
Texas	College Station	WTAW	1620 AM

State	Market(s)	Station	Frequency
Texas	Edinburg	KURV	710 AM
Texas	El Paso	KTSM	690 AM
Texas	Fort Worth	WBAP	820 AM
Texas	Houston	KPRC	950 AM
Texas	Rollingwood	KJCE	1370 AM
Texas	Texarkana	KTFS	940 AM
Texas	Tyler	KTBB	600 AM
Utah	Cedar City	KSUB	590 AM
Utah	Logan	KVNU	610 AM
Utah	Salt Lake City	KNRS	570 AM
Utah	St. George	KDXU	890 AM
Vermont	Rutland	WSYB	1380 AM
Virginia	Abingdon	WFHG	92.7 FM
Virginia	Glen Allen	WTOX	1480 AM
Virginia	Martinsville	WHEE	1370 AM
Virginia	Norfolk	WNIS	790 AM
Washington	Moses Lake	KBSN	1470 AM
Washington	Port Angeles	KONP	1450 AM
Washington	Pullman	KQQQ	1150 AM
Washington	Seattle	KIRO	710 AM
Washington	Spokane	KXLY	920 AM
Washington	Wenatchee	KPQ	560 AM
Washington, D.C.	Washington	WMAL	630 AM
West Virginia	Charleston	WVTS	950 AM
Wisconsin	Amery	WXCE	1260 AM
Wisconsin	Green Bay	WTAQ	1360 AM
Wisconsin	La Crosse	WIZM	1410 AM
Wisconsin	Wausau	WSAU	550 AM

Let me close with three rules for the active trader:

1. The less you do, the less can go wrong.
2. If you are in a financial hole, stop digging.
3. If you want to learn from your financial mistakes, stop making them.

May the gods of trading smile upon your countenance.